M000215329

SMART,
NOT
LOUD

SMART, NOT LOUD

*How to Get Noticed at Work
for All the Right Reasons*

JESSICA CHEN

PORTFOLIO | PENGUIN

Portfolio / Penguin
An imprint of Penguin Random House LLC
penguinrandomhouse.com

Copyright © 2024 by Jessica Chen
Penguin Random House supports copyright. Copyright fuels creativity,
encourages diverse voices, promotes free speech, and creates a vibrant culture.
Thank you for buying an authorized edition of this book and for complying
with copyright laws by not reproducing, scanning, or distributing any part of
it in any form without permission. You are supporting writers and allowing
Penguin Random House to continue to publish books for every reader.

Most Portfolio books are available at a discount when purchased in quantity for
sales promotions or corporate use. Special editions, which include personalized
covers, excerpts, and corporate imprints, can be created when purchased in
large quantities. For more information, please call (212) 572-2232 or e-mail
specialmarkets@penguinrandomhouse.com. Your local bookstore can also
assist with discounted bulk purchases using the Penguin Random House
corporate Business-to-Business program. For assistance in locating a
participating retailer, e-mail B2B@penguinrandomhouse.com.

Library of Congress Cataloging-in-Publication Data

Names: Chen, Jessica (CEO of Soulcast media), author.
Title: Smart, not loud : how to get noticed at work for all the
right reasons / Jessica Chen.
Description: [New York] : Portfolio/Penguin, [2024] |
Includes bibliographical references and index. |
Identifiers: LCCN 2024004158 (print) | LCCN 2024004159 (ebook) |
ISBN 9780593717684 (hardcover) | ISBN 9780593717691 (ebook)
Subjects: LCSH: Communication in management. | Success in business. |
Work—Psychological aspects. | Employee morale.
Classification: LCC HD30.3 .C4557 2024 (print) | LCC HD30.3 (ebook) |
DDC 658.4/5—dc23/eng/20240319
LC record available at https://lccn.loc.gov/2024004158
LC ebook record available at https://lccn.loc.gov/2024004159

Printed in the United States of America
1st Printing

Book design by Nicole LaRoche

Some names and identifying characteristics have been changed
to protect the privacy of the individuals involved.

For my family

CONTENTS

PREFACE

When I first conceptualized this book, it was supposed to be a tactical communication guide for Asian Americans in the workplace. However, the more I worked on it, the more I realized the struggles and friction I wanted to highlight were felt by many people around the world. Feelings of being overlooked, voiceless, and invisible resonated everywhere. But more important, these feelings could be attributed to some of the values and beliefs we were raised to embrace. This book is for those who were raised with "quiet" traits but are now working in a "loud" world. It's for those who want to find a way of showing up and getting noticed at work without losing a part of themselves in the process.

In writing this book, generalizations have been made about Quiet Cultures and Loud Cultures. The concepts of "quiet" and "loud" are painted in broad strokes and are actually much more nuanced than what's outlined. It's important to note, whether you were raised with quiet or loud traits, *one is not better than the other*. Both are equally valued and needed. Also, the way we show up and how we feel at work are influenced by more than just the way we were raised. This book does not cover those additional influences, nor does it dive into the prejudices, biases, and bullying that can make being seen and heard much more difficult.

Names have been changed throughout to protect people's identities. Where affiliations are identified, I have used the actual names of individuals who were interviewed and shared their experience.

INTRODUCTION

Kevin, a junior associate at a large consumer brand, entered his boss's office, burdened by an overwhelming feeling of disappointment. He was unable to comprehend why he had been passed over for a promotion he had been eagerly anticipating. Determined to get to the root of the matter, he approached his boss, Ben, and asked the question that had been weighing on his mind: "You liked my work; how come I didn't get the promotion?"

Ben, who had been busy juggling several pressing matters, turned to Kevin and responded, "Let me show you something."

He strode over to the whiteboard in his office, took hold of a dry-erase marker, and drew several circles. "Within each circle are the things going on in my life right now," Ben explained. "I'm thinking about my own promotion. I'm thinking about my client who is upset at me. I'm thinking about my wife who wants me to go to a dinner event with her. I'm thinking about my dog that just injured his leg. I'm thinking about my kids and their upcoming baseball game. I have thirty employees, three of whom are always coming into my office, making small talk." He paused, then continued, "You don't come into my office, so how often do you think I'm going to think about you when I have all these things occupying my brain?"

Kevin stood there, stunned. He had never thought about it that way. He figured his work would—and should—speak for itself.

"I like you a lot," Ben added. "I know you have a lot of potential, but you need to proactively come into my office and make your presence part of my daily brain."

This story was shared by my friend Michael Chen as we were chatting on Zoom one afternoon about what it takes to find workplace success today. Chen is the former president and CEO of General Electric's Media, Communications, and Entertainment division. As Chen shared this story, I couldn't help but reflect that I could relate to Kevin's plight.

Growing up, I was never taught the importance of making myself visible, of continually following up as a way of staying top of mind. I was never taught the importance of being proactive or how to speak up with tact. Instead, I was taught to work hard, hit my key performance indicators, and not cause trouble. The expectation was that as long as I did these things, promotions and raises would follow, like clockwork. However, as with Kevin, it didn't take long for me to see that this formula wasn't actually what was needed to be successful in the workplace. What actually mattered was the ability to showcase myself. Not only that, communication and being visible were *required*—and rewarded. Thus, a paradox started to form. How was I supposed to be "loud" when I was only ever taught to embody more "quiet" traits?

I've discovered there's a group of us today who were raised in what I call a Quiet Culture. People like us are told from an early age to follow instructions, listen to others, talk less, and let our work speak for itself. But those raised in a Loud Culture are taught to do virtually the opposite: share their opinions frequently, make a lot of noise, and carve out opportunities for themselves. One is not better than the other, but when one cultural context is placed in another, the ability to get noticed in a way that feels right becomes difficult.

Early on, when I started to feel stuck at work, I immersed myself in learning, listening, and reading all the communication and leadership content out there to glean insight into how to become more loud and visible. While insightful, many of the teachings didn't address my most pressing question: Could I still hold on to my Quiet Culture values, or did I need to mold myself and become a loud person to fit in? And if I didn't, would I just become utterly forgotten?

As I began to look around, one of the most surprising things I found was that I wasn't alone in feeling this way. Many people, like me, who were raised with Quiet Culture values felt unsure about how to chime in or show up in a Loud Culture working world. They also felt like they didn't know how to do it without acting a certain way. It's why I have dedicated this book to talking about Quiet Culture and Loud Culture. Specifically, this book is for those who were raised with Quiet Culture traits and are now working in a Loud Culture world. Because the truth is, this friction goes beyond just being an introvert or extrovert; it's something deeper. It's the values and beliefs we have been taught in our most formative years that have shaped who we've become, what we know, and what behaviors we find comfort in.

This book is a guide, a dedication, and a personal reflection of sorts that explores the question I hoped to answer years ago. Over time, I have discovered that it *is* possible to be noticed exactly the way we want to be without complete acculturation. We can still honor that Quiet Culture part of our nature while expanding what we know, how we act, and how we communicate, so we can better express ourselves in the workplace today. This is what part 1 of this book is about. We will dive deeper into the two worlds of Quiet Culture and Loud Culture, and we will unveil what each looks like. We will also talk about how to find a cultural balance through what I call our Cultural Reframes, which will help us rethink how we engage with others, spend our time at work, handle wins, and manage conflict. I don't discount the fact that there is such a thing as a Quiet Culture bias that exists in the workplace, so we will spend time talking about it, including sharing tips on how to overcome it—specifically the things we tell ourselves. Because, as the saying goes, we can't keep doing the same thing over and over and expect different results. We need a new road map.

From there, we enter part 2 of the book, which takes our reframes and gives them legs. I call this step implementing our Quiet Capital Framework, a three-pillar structure that allows us to be seen exactly the way we want. The three pillars are: shaping our career brand, establishing credibility, and advocating for ourselves. We will go over, step-by-step, how to apply these pillars to our daily work. Because the truth is, if we don't control the narrative of how people perceive us and what others think of us, the opportunities we get will be left to chance.

With every great plan comes hopefully even better execution. Part 3 is where we will talk about communication skills. This section will feel very tactical, and that's the intent. We will go over practical communication strategies and show you what to say and how to say it at work. It's also set up so that if you ever need tips for giving presentations, using body language, or refining your speaking, you can just turn to the right page. Because in my work helping people build their communication confidence, I have discovered that even though we may know the techniques for getting noticed, if we can't *deliver* well, then our impact is much less powerful. In other words, no matter how much we know or how much we plan, none of it will matter unless it lands.

PRIOR TO STARTING my global communication training company, Soulcast Media, I was a broadcast television journalist for nearly ten years. Winning an Emmy Award at ABC in San Diego was the culmination of my career in news, and it was the catalyst that propelled me to start my own company. One of the reasons why, after I left TV, I entered the risky world of business was because I saw that many of the tactics I learned about communications and speaking up at work could be applied in the broader professional world. Witnessing the most eloquent speakers present seamlessly, navigate tricky conversations with tact, and eloquently advocate for themselves was like taking a master class in effective communication. It was a mindset shift coupled with tactics, both of which pointed to being smart, not loud. So in studying the great TV journalists and applying the strategies myself, I found the answer I was looking for: you can *absolutely* be noticed for all the right reasons without needing to be loud.

Since starting Soulcast Media, I have heard from countless leaders and professionals who have appreciated the acknowledgment of Quiet Culture traits while existing in a Loud Culture workplace, and the point of friction this has created. I frequently receive notes like this one: "I too grew up in a culture that emphasized modesty, keeping your head down and working. But, as you've pointed out before, those are not necessarily the best tips when you're trying to succeed at the office. I've read books and taken courses about how to overcome these mental barriers, but I've never heard the acknowledgment [of this cultural friction] and have never taken advice from someone whom I related with. I think that was the key. I took [your advice] to heart and simply applied some of these 'gold nugget' tips." Those gold nuggets are now in this book, and they're meant to give you a new way forward too.

In fact, even if you were raised in a Loud Culture household but resonate more with Quiet Culture traits, this book will provide a road map for how you too can build influence. It can also be for those who identify as having been raised in a Loud Culture but want to better understand the thinking of those raised with Quiet Culture values. Perhaps, in reading this, we can also begin to shift how people perceive those raised with Quiet Culture traits to create a more inclusive workplace. It is important to note, though, that this book is not meant to be the one solution to a complicated and layered workplace experience. But it will shed light on some of the unspoken and often silent dynamics at play.

Today, I am honored to have impacted millions of people around the world. My courses on LinkedIn Learning are consistently ranked among the most popular and have been watched by more than two million people, many of whom are global leaders. I'm frequently invited to speak at Fortune 100 companies to teach and inspire teams to better show up, engage, and stand out in a hypercompetitive business environment. When I reflect back to that person who struggled with showing up and sharing her ideas at work, I can still see her, because it's not about completely changing who we are. Rather, it's about taking our Quiet Culture values and reframing them so we get noticed for all the right reasons. Now you will be able to do that too.

SMART,
NOT
LOUD

PART 1

CULTURE
SHOCK

Our most formative years, our childhood years, are often shaped by our family and our friends. It's in these environments where we're often taught a set of principles that's meant to guide us on how to behave and engage. But what if these principles are now causing us to feel stuck, like we're living in a confusing world where cultures clash? Chances are it's because we are viewing the world through our Quiet Culture lens, while the workplace is rewarding those who exhibit Loud Culture traits. In part 1, we explore what these cultural differences are, the Quiet Culture bias, and how we can reframe this friction so we can navigate the working world with greater ease.

CHAPTER 1

FRICTION AT WORK

Stuck between two cultures

One of the earliest memories I have of growing up is being sprawled on the carpet with the ten o'clock evening news playing in the background. My brother is next to me, and my parents are sitting on the couch behind us attentively watching the news. For years, this nightly ritual was somewhat of a family tradition as we all ended the day watching television together.

"Jessica, when you grow up one day, you should talk on the news just like them," my mom said, pointing to the reporters on TV one night.

"But why?" I responded.

"So I can see where you are and make sure you are safe every day," my mom replied with a half smile.

To a six-year-old, this seemingly innocent, lighthearted comment didn't mean much at the time, but fifteen years later, I found myself exactly where my mom had hoped: in TV news. In the years leading up to graduation, like many young college students, I was beginning to think about the question *What do you want to do for your career?* For students around the world, this loaded question induces sleepless nights of stress and anxiety. But for me, the moment I started exploring the possibility of journalism being a career, I was convinced it was the right path for me. Everything about it—learning about different industries, being at the heart of the action, and telling stories in hopes of making the world a better place—pulled me in like nothing else could. So, that spark of an idea my mom planted in me that fateful night had now grown into a roaring fire. This career felt like destiny.

Just a few months after finishing school, I landed my first job in Reno, Nevada, as a television news reporter. It was the beginning of what I anticipated would be a storied career in journalism. However, as proud as I was to have locked in what became my dream job, I knew there was a lot more work to do. Because I not only wanted to be a journalist, I wanted to be the *best* journalist. So, I spent every waking hour learning, studying, and practicing. At work, I attentively listened to everything my bosses told me to do, soaking in every bit of advice they gave. After work, I stayed late to dig through documents in hopes of finding hidden stories that were overlooked. On the weekends, I picked up books written by former journalists to glean insight into how *they* had succeeded. And if I really wanted to feel inspired, I would watch and rewatch my favorite TV anchors on air because I was convinced that if I worked hard enough, I would be just like them one day. I lived and breathed journalism.

However, it didn't take long for me to see that a paradox was beginning to form. Despite working hard, I was still not getting the bigger and better opportunities at work. I was getting stuck doing the most basic projects, and I couldn't figure out why. For example, when an exciting story came into our newsroom and I expressed my interest, I would immediately see it be handed off to someone else. Initially, I chalked it up to being new, but as newer employees joined after me, I noticed I was still being offered the less desirable projects. That feeling of being slighted, left out, and even invisible started to creep in. I thought, if I'm doing everything I am supposed to do, including putting in the hours and listening to all the instructions given to me, why am I being overlooked? The balance between what I was expecting and what was happening was off, and I needed to figure out why.

This conundrum came to a head in 2010, a few months after I started my first job. One day, our newsroom got notice that in two weeks, the US Air Force Air Demonstration Squadron, the "Thunderbirds," would be coming into town. They were hosting an air show, and as part of their PR campaign, they would allow one reporter to fly with them.

Excited about the prospect of flying in a high-speed aircraft reserved only for those in the military, I raised my hand and mentioned to my boss that I would love to do the story.

"OK, noted," he said. I walked away from the meeting with a smile on my face, and I mentally patted myself on the back for finding the courage to express what I wanted.

For two whole weeks, I fantasized about how I would put

the story together and what an extraordinary opportunity this would be.

On the day of the air show, reporters and producers filed into the conference room to start our daily editorial meeting. I sat in my seat and waited for my boss to announce the plan for the air show.

"As for who will be covering the story, Bella will be riding with them."

Immediately, my head swiveled to my boss. My heart dropped to the pit of my stomach. I was sure my face showed it. Without even looking at me, my boss continued on with the day's agenda as if I were completely invisible. The feeling of "my" story being handed off to someone else was gut-wrenching.

At the end of the meeting, despite feeling incredibly uncomfortable, I mustered up the courage to ask my boss why someone else had been assigned the story.

"Just curious," I said in my least disappointed-sounding voice. "Why is Bella covering the story? I was really hoping to do it."

My boss looked up at me, seemingly confused.

"Oh, that's right," he responded. "I forgot you had mentioned it! Bella was interested in it, and she was just talking about it all week, so she was top of mind. Sorry—next time!"

I knew there would be no next time, but nothing could be done now.

As I walked back to my desk, I kept ruminating over his words: "top of mind"; "talking about it all week."

In the two weeks leading up to the air show, I had thought about following up and reminding him of my interest. But because I hadn't wanted to intrude or bother him, I'd decided against it. Moreover, I didn't know how to approach being *top of mind* without seeming pushy. Therein was the friction: because I didn't know what to do or how to do it, I simply did nothing.

As I walked back to my desk that fateful day, ruminating over my manager's words, I knew something had to change. So I put on my journalist hat and started investigating. I asked myself a multitude of questions, like: Why did I think asking for something once was enough? Why did I assume he would remember? Why did I default to thinking I'd inconvenience him if I followed up? The more I looked into it, the more I realized my attempts at being noticed, remembered, and recognized were futile. Not only that, I was getting in my own head, creating a narrative of what I thought would happen, including being negatively perceived as pushy or annoying, or even getting downright rejected. The question of "What's there to lose?" was, for me, imagining the pitfalls, consequences, and risk. But it wasn't just that; I felt myself, more often than not, suppressing what I wanted to say in meetings. My mind would race with negative thoughts, causing me to doubt myself and my expertise.

At first, I attributed these feelings to my personality. Maybe it was because I was more introverted, shy, and timid; therefore, it was harder for me to communicate. However, the more

I looked into it, the more I began to see it was more than personality alone. For instance, I didn't consider myself soft-spoken or anxious when I was around my family and friends, but when I was in a professional environment, it was like I suddenly was. Deep down, I knew there were bigger forces at play that caused me to stay quiet, downplay my thoughts, question my capabilities, and acquiesce. Over time, I discovered it was because I was showing up in the workplace exhibiting the Quiet Culture traits I had been raised with, but the workplace was expecting something else.

QUIET CULTURE VS. LOUD CULTURE

In my years working with professionals to help them communicate more confidently in the workplace, I have discovered that there is indeed a group of people who gravitate toward thinking and behaving with "quiet" traits. For example, listening rather than talking in meetings. Following directions rather than engaging in discussion. Advocating for others, but not advocating for themselves. Deflecting attention and praise. Having a more risk-averse mentality, in which they tend to stay within the confines of what they know. Those of us who come from Quiet Cultures are often seen as "the quiet one" at work.

On the flip side, those who come from Loud Cultures often prefer speaking over staying silent. They are taught to engage in discourse and to see rules, processes, and structure as open to interpretation. They don't consider confrontation disrespectful, but think of it as a way to show their thought process. Those who behave with "loud" traits also don't shy away from talking about their work, their impact, and their accomplishments. In the Western world, corporate workplaces tend to reward those who exhibit "loud" behaviors, because work emphasizes individualism, self-determination, and autonomy.

But how did it become this way? Why do Western companies, as well as many global workplaces, now value Loud Culture traits? It helps to look at how Western society was formed thousands of years ago. The philosophical underpinnings that shaped Western democracies are rooted in Greek ideology. From the likes of Aristotle to Plato, these philosophers talked about individualism—one's ability to carve out their own path, speak their mind, and create their own future. In fact, the ability to express one's ideas, discuss them openly, and challenge others was not only expected, it was rewarded. Psychologist Richard E. Nisbett writes in his book *The Geography of Thought* this poignant example: "The Greek sense of agency fueled a tradition of debate. . . . A commoner could challenge even a king and not only live to tell the tale, but occasionally sway an audience to his side." If we translate this into workspeak, we can see a young employee rise up fast in the corporate world because they're not only good at what they do, but they're not afraid to challenge the status quo, seize opportunities, and take on projects others might not want to do. They speak their mind and put themselves out there and are not discouraged from doing it; rather, they are praised for it.

In fact, we don't have to look very far to see where these characteristics are embedded in Western companies today. The importance of successfully making oneself known can be found in the value statements of some of the most renowned businesses. Amazon's core leadership principles outline an expectation for employees to think big, which means being able to communicate a bold direction that inspires results. They want their employees to have a "backbone" and to openly "disagree and commit." The payroll-software company Gusto lists "Debate then commit" as one of its five values highlighted on its website, and the fintech company Enova has on its culture page a quote from an engineering lead saying the company's ability to innovate is because of the motto "Be Bold and Move Fast." In 2009, Google conducted a study that showed the mark of a great leader in today's world is not technical expertise, but the ability to converse, ask questions, and help others solve problems. Specifically, in American culture, we see companies push their team to enter the market quickly to gain what experts call a first-mover advantage, in which people and organizations vie to be first to the marketplace to gain a competitive advantage. While there is research that states being the first is not as advantageous as one would think, people still push their teams to be the most innovative, and the market elevates those who are the most disruptive with awards and accolades. In other words, if we want to succeed in the

Western workplace, we have to embody what these companies expect: be assertive and communicative.

However, for me, being bold and unapologetically forthright in a professional setting was not an easy thing to do. I grew up in an environment where the overarching sentiment was to keep to oneself and become invisible as a means of survival. When my parents emigrated from Taiwan to the US, they carried with them little to nothing. Their move to a new country was a fresh start, but the only guarantee was that they *might* be able to build a better future for themselves and their family. So, from day one, they got to work quickly, quietly, and diligently. Values such as stability over risk-taking, saving over indulgence, and safety over unpredictability governed everything they did and the decisions they made. It was also what they expected of us, their kids. When my brother and I were growing up, they taught us to embody their same mentality and beliefs. They reinforced that these were the traits needed to succeed.

Whether our Quiet Culture values come from the community we were born into, our ethnic background, or even the temperament of our parents, many of us get our first inkling of the Quiet and Loud Culture difference the moment we start working. This is what researchers call organizational socialization, and it's the process by which we begin learning new norms and the behaviors and skills that are expected of us. As we experience things like onboarding training, being paired with a workplace mentor, or just observing how people carry themselves in meetings, we start to internalize these spoken and unspoken rules. Soon, we begin to see there are a set of be-haviors that feel contrary to what comes naturally to us.

To see these in more detail, let's lay them out in the four areas where the differences are most distinct. I call them the Cultural Dualities at Work.

CULTURAL DUALITIES AT WORK

	QUIET CULTURE	LOUD CULTURE
Engage Others: *How we communicate*	Listen more than speak	Participate by discussing and challenging
Spend Time: *How we prefer to work*	Put our heads down and work hard	Spend time building connections
Handle Wins: *How we celebrate our achievements*	Be humble and don't boast	Ensure others notice our accomplishments
Manage Conflict: *How we handle tricky situations*	Avoid conflict to maintain a harmonious environment	Address problems openly and honestly

When you look at the dualities from a bird's-eye view, you can see that within each of the four areas of Engage Others, Spend Time, Handle Wins, and Manage Conflict, there is a drastic difference between Quiet Culture and Loud Culture behaviors. Let's look at each one in more detail, beginning with Engage Others. This is how people communicate at work. For those of us who resonate with Quiet Culture traits, our natural mode of communicating is to default to listening more than speaking. We were taught growing up that it's better to listen to others and to follow what is said. We were also told that if we did need to say something, we should either wait until the very end or do it discreetly so we wouldn't draw attention to ourselves. And if we need clarification, we should ask for it only by raising our hands to signal our interest, and to pose it as a question so we don't offend others. On the opposite side, those who resonate with Loud Culture traits communicate with a level of fluidity and ease. They embody a sense of self-confidence when speaking, believing it's better to share their thoughts and add in their two cents than stay silent in meetings. If a manager is in the room, they also don't feel like they have to agree with everything the manager says. Instead, they see authority as a guide, someone who can be swayed. They don't shy away from discussing, debating, and even challenging others. In fact, Western workplaces value those who speak up so much that these people are generally perceived as having more leadership qualities. One study found the quality of the thought didn't even matter; it was about the quantity of speaking. Researchers call this the babble hypothesis.

The next Cultural Duality is Spend Time, which is how we prefer to work. Those of us who resonate with a Quiet Culture were told to quietly work hard and to do as we were told. The promise was that as long as we diligently put in the hours, we would get rewarded for our efforts. Furthermore, we were told to focus on sharpening our technical and analytical skills, because these skills would position us to be experts in our field. So, we stayed close to the numbers and books, instead of spending time developing the soft skills of work, such as building interpersonal relationships and effective speaking. On the flip side, those from a Loud Culture view spending time as not just doing the work but also working on projects that can maximize their influence. They get things done, but they also spend time socializing, attending events, making small talk, and increasing connections, internally and externally. Those who embody Loud Culture traits see time as well spent if they can build stronger working relationships, even if the return on investment isn't measured in data or dollars.

Next is Handle Wins, which is how we carry ourselves and celebrate our achievements. Those of us who come from a Quiet Culture were told to stay humble and to not boast. If something great happens to us at work, we deflect the praise, minimize our role, and redirect the acknowledgment. We do feel happy about the recognition, but we find it hard to talk about our accomplishments and promote ourselves in front of others. In fact, when we do good work, we trust that others will just notice it, and that our work will speak for itself. However, those from a Loud Culture revel more openly in their accomplishments. They find multiple ways to talk about their work, and they do so proudly and outwardly. They carry themselves with an air of confidence, and they maximize their visibility, because they want to use every achievement as an opportunity to stay front and center.

And finally, there's Manage Conflict, which is how we handle tricky situations at work. For those of us who were raised in a Quiet Culture, creating and maintaining a harmonious environment was often emphasized. We were told to avoid conflict and to shy away from engaging in any sort of dialogue that could lead to confrontation. So, if something negative comes up, we quickly acquiesce in order to resolve the tension, even though we might not fully agree with what's going on. Or we try to handle the situation by ourselves to avoid disturbing people and the environment. However, those from Loud Cultures don't shy away from addressing tricky situations head-on. While it may not be the most comfortable for them, they don't necessarily see conflict as a bad thing. They see it as something that needs to be addressed in order to move things forward.

THE CULTURAL SCALE

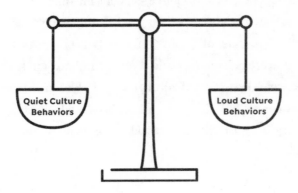

At first glance, it's easy to see Quiet and Loud Cultures as binary concepts. If we were raised in a Quiet Culture environment, we can only behave with Quiet Culture traits, and so on. But the truth is, Quiet Culture and Loud Culture behaviors are like a balance scale. We can find ourselves exhibiting Loud Culture traits even if we grew up with Quiet Culture values, and vice versa. Circumstances, including who we are around, what's happening, and how comfortable we feel, all affect how we act in the moment. There will be times when chiming in during meetings quickly, addressing conflict head-on, or choosing to make ourselves visible will come easily. In fact, there may be situations in which we will feel like we have no other choice but to exhibit Loud Culture traits, because we feel strongly about the topic. So we put our Quiet Culture tendencies aside and do what we need to do to get the job done.

For example, think about when you're around certain colleagues you like—how much easier is it for you to share your thoughts, engage, and build relationships with them? Or if you have a work project and you see someone misinterpreting your results, how instinctive is it for you to jump in and clarify the point? It's a scale, and sometimes we will be pulled toward Loud Culture behaviors, while at other times we will find ourselves grounded in Quiet Culture traits. It's like an ocean wave: sometimes we will deliberately pull back, and sometimes we will surge forward with power and strength.

Quiet by Nurture

There are so many aspects of our upbringing that can lead us to identify as coming from a Quiet Culture. Some of us were taught to embody traditional roles and values, perhaps through religion or gender expectations. Perhaps it was the community we were raised in, where if we exerted ourselves in any loud way we would be perceived unfavorably, which shaped our behavior. Or, maybe there was a household emphasis on it being the *polite* thing to do, so we made way for others first, putting our thoughts second. How we came to embody these quiet values is a part of our story today.

For Maggie Wagner, the reason she resonated with Quiet Culture values was attributed to her parents' temperament and the way they wanted their home environment to be.

"I wouldn't say we were taught to hate loudness, but that was sort of what happened," Maggie said.

Being raised in a small town in Indiana, she said she was most used to being in a quiet home around quiet people. For example, if she or a member of her family spoke, it was always with a hushed tone of voice. If music was playing, it was on ambient sound. If the television was on, it was like background noise, on low. Her home was this way, she said, because her parents wanted to create a "peaceful" environment.

"My mom's upbringing was pretty chaotic. It wasn't peaceful, so I think her desire, when she had kids, was to basically provide the safest possible place," said Maggie. "My father is very reserved and cerebral, so the combination of those two things made it so we were taught to be respectful and reverent."

However, for Maggie, this quiet way of being and communicating was in stark contrast to the fast-paced world she was now operating in. Working at a large publishing house in New York City, she found she needed to make decisions quickly, to rush and hit deadlines, and to advocate for herself and her ideas. For Maggie, speaking up and making herself known, especially in front of her senior editors, her publicity team, and her managers, felt like a mystery.

"I think there is a lot of confrontation in the corporate world, and that has really been my biggest obstacle, because that was not something I learned growing up," she said. "I hated the idea of discussing anything that was going to put me in a vulnerable position."

Over time, Maggie said, she began to look more deeply at the behaviors she was used to versus the ones that were recognized at work. But it wasn't about judging which one was better; it was about seeing the behaviors in the right context. So instead of always erring on the side of being quiet, Maggie had to learn that she could talk about her work, especially if she was proud of it, in order to make others aware. Instead of muting her accomplishments, she could show she was smart and capable, and know that it wasn't self-serving to do so. And instead of thinking her contributions weren't as important, she had to trust that she brought just as much value to the team as the person next to her.

"Learning how to push myself, which is growth, is how I am tackling it."

WORD TO THE WISE

 There is no question that the way we were raised affects how we show up in the workplace today. According to developmental psychologists, "The things we have learned are determined by the demands of the environment in which we grew up." As young children, we internalize specific rules, behaviors, and wisdom. We consciously and unconsciously allow this to shape who we become, including how we communicate and engage with others. Anthropologists call this social learning, and it starts the moment we're born. As you reflect on how you've come to resonate with Quiet Culture behaviors, try pinpointing whether it could be certain principles your parents taught you that shaped your behaviors now. Were there sayings they reiterated? Stories they told you? Reflecting on your younger years is how you can better understand how you show up today.

Helen Grayson, a forensic scientist working at one of the busiest crime labs in the country, said that while she resonates with Quiet Culture traits, spending time building her network and making connections with her colleagues, including her manager, feels natural to her at work.

"We go out for lunch all the time, we go for coffee runs, and I even [grab food] with my manager, so we have a pretty good working relationship," she said.

However, for Grayson, the reality of not knowing what to say in a Loud Culture became glaringly evident the moment she was being interviewed for a leadership position at work. Sitting face-to-face with her manager, a person she was comfortable with, Grayson said she suddenly felt like she couldn't articulate her accomplishments in a clear and intentional way.

"It was difficult and unnatural for me to talk about my abilities so explicitly and directly without feeling like I was showing off or being boastful," said Grayson.

Grayson said she defaulted to her Quiet Culture traits, minimized her accomplishments and spoke little of her technical abilities. She didn't even mention her leadership aspirations, which was why she wanted the job in the first place. Instead, she thought the sheer number of hours she spent in the lab every day and the results she produced were evidence enough of how capable she was.

"I assumed that because she knew me and she knew my work, that was all that mattered. However, I didn't get the job, because she was expecting me to talk about my skills and my abilities in a more confident way. I failed to mention my many achievements over the years," said Grayson. "This was the feedback I got after I lost the position to another candidate."

What Grayson experienced is not unlike what many of us

Quiet Culture professionals feel in a Loud Culture workplace. We will be talking to someone we are comfortable with, but because our environment is more formal or the stakes are higher, we feel like we have to carry ourselves in an entirely different way. We freeze up, minimize our expertise, and don't know what to say even though we know our stuff. Or, more specifically, because we are less in control, we don't know where our voice fits in. So we default to saying nothing, just to stay on the safe side.

Recognizing when our Quiet Culture values may mute us and cause us to take a back seat is the first step in taking control. Because in order for us to be noticed the way we want to be, we have to know when and how to show up and speak up in *all* environments, and in front of *all* people. How we reframe the way we show up will be the key to creating more visibility at work while staying true to ourselves.

THE POWER OF QUIET CULTURES

It's important to note, the power of those raised with Quiet Culture values cannot be underestimated. Listening, keeping our head down, staying humble, and avoiding conflict are necessary attributes to balance out a Loud Culture workplace. Because when we know how to turn off the noise, put our head down, and get things done, we move the needle forward. When we know how to stay humble, we open ourselves to diverse ways of thinking. When we know how to avoid conflict, we find alternate ways of solving problems that minimize disruption. And when everyone is speaking over each other, we know how to read the room and pick up on the unspoken dynamics at play.

All these are powerful attributes of a Quiet Culture person, not just at work, but in society as a whole. Without professionals raised with Quiet Culture values, we would be living in a world filled with a cacophony of ideas that would be so distracting, it would be hard to get anything done. So the key isn't to diminish these behaviors that come naturally to us, but rather to *expand* how we show up. Because the truth is, our approach, our beliefs, and our nature are valued and are needed too.

What is also powerful about those who exhibit Quiet Culture traits, especially in a Loud Culture workplace, is the amount of courage and resilience that is practiced every day. For Quiet Culture professionals, being asked to show up and engage in a workplace where the expectation of how to act is different from the values we find comfort in can be scary, stressful, and intimidating. It can also be frustrating, and even confusing at times, to live within the tension between these two cultures. To deal with competing ideologies of what we *think* versus what is *expected* can be overwhelming and can be an added mental stress on top of the everyday pressures at work. But despite it all, we still show up and do our best. We do it not because anyone told us to, but because we know it'll help us become stronger versions of ourselves.

Above all, the power of those raised with quiet values isn't just our resilience or our ability to be attuned to the more quiet attributes of work; it's also our perspective. To understand both worlds is, in my opinion, a true superpower. By juggling the dualities between Quiet Cultures and Loud Cultures, we can see the value of both approaches. We can dance between the two and know that there are many ways to engage and get things done, and there is no one right way. So, the power is our ability to embrace and honor both cultures, because they enrich the person we are. It's not about which is better, it's about context and navigating the world with more fluidity and ease.

WHAT'S NEXT?

Success in the workplace isn't about being loud if we're quiet. Success is about finding a balance between our Quiet Culture upbringing and Loud Culture environment, so we can get noticed for all the right reasons. It's about finding an authentic communication style that works for us and doubling down on our innate human desire to connect. It's thinking about strategy, especially when stakes are high. So instead of getting lost in our own heads and wondering whether we should or should not put ourselves out there, the better question is: How can we reframe the four Cultural Dualities at Work so they serve us better?

THE BOTTOM LINE

- We experience friction in the workplace when our jobs require us to exhibit Loud Culture traits but we exemplify Quiet Culture behaviors.

- Those who were raised in a Quiet Culture would rather listen than speak. They prefer to put their head down and work hard, be humble about their achievements, and not rock the boat.

- Those who were raised in a Loud Culture prefer speaking and discussing. They would rather build connections, ensure others notice their work, and not shy away from addressing conflict.

- There are four main areas where we can experience friction in the workplace, called the Cultural Dualities at Work: how we engage and communicate with others, how we spend our time at work, how we celebrate our achievements, and how we manage conflict.

- Where we fall on the Cultural Scale depends on our environment, who is there, and how comfortable we feel.

- The power of Quiet Culture professionals is the courage and resilience we practice every day.

CHAPTER 2

THE FOUR CULTURAL REFRAMES

Seeking a cultural balance

When my mother's family immigrated to the United States from Taiwan, one of the first things they did was establish a Chinese restaurant in Newark, California. My father helped set up the restaurant and named it Peach Garden. In Chinese culture, peaches symbolize longevity, which in his mind was an auspicious sign for what he hoped would happen for the business, his family, and future generations. But practically speaking, this business was created for the purpose of survival. Starting a restaurant would ensure that members of our family—my aunts and uncles—would all have jobs. It was a surefire way to provide income and job security, and keep the family close.

With the family's restaurant established, my aunts and uncles began divvying up roles. My uncles took the positions in the kitchen and cooked up Chinese dishes that reflected the taste of their American clientele, such as chow fun, beef and broccoli, and sweet-and-sour soup. Meanwhile my aunts—at least the ones who spoke decent English—staffed the front of the restaurant, answered the phone, and took customer orders. Everyone fell naturally into their roles and responsibilities because everyone knew what was expected of them, including how to act, when to speak, and who to listen to. The unspoken rules for how to behave, communicate, and engage pointed to a shared understanding of Quiet Culture values.

However, many of us in the workforce today are not operating in a setting surrounded by family. We are in an environment that is largely driven by competition and market share, and we are faced with juggling fickle personalities and demanding clients every single day. Our Quiet Culture approach may now feel out of place because Loud Culture behaviors are expected. But the point isn't for us to judge which is better or worse; it is to learn how we can position ourselves to be noticed the way we want to be. Because the truth is, if we are raised with Quiet Culture values and we stay firmly rooted in them while our workplace is a Loud Culture environment, we will become utterly invisible. On the other hand, if we try to mold ourselves to behave only with Loud Culture traits, our actions will feel completely inauthentic to who we are.

So here is where the lesson begins. In the following sections, we will go over the four Cultural Dualities at Work, the friction we experience because of these dualities, and the Cultural Reframes that will help us build our superpower so we feel more balanced.

ENGAGE OTHERS:
HOW WE COMMUNICATE

CULTURAL REFRAME

Tailor your message to what
your audience cares about

Jamie Chung couldn't quite shake the feeling of being confused and frustrated. Despite working hard and doing everything she could to please her boss, every time they met, their conversation was littered with communication friction.

"Boy, we were not getting along," said Chung, who is now the chief corporate counsel at Rivian, an electric vehicle manufacturer. But early on at her first job out of law school, she said she was having a hard time engaging with her boss, and she couldn't figure out why.

As a young attorney, Chung was doing all the work that was required of her. She was preparing briefs, drafting memos, and preparing detailed notes to give her manager. Despite it all, she felt like the work wasn't being appreciated or even recognized the way she wanted it to be. Many of us who were raised in a Quiet Culture may experience a similar kind of communication friction. We work hard, we follow instructions, and we get things in on time, but when we start talking about our work, we feel like our efforts don't truly shine through. One of the reasons for this is the way we were taught to talk about our work. For example, we think we have to share all the data and facts to prove we know our stuff. But what others may want is just two or three high-level points to help them make an informed decision. Or we think because we are experts in our field, when we tell people what we know, they will get it instantly—but instead, what they want is why this information matters to them. So a better way to engage others at work is to not just passively listen, mute our thoughts, or brain-dump everything at once; it's to think about whom we're speaking with and what *they* care about.

So the Cultural Reframe for Engage Others is: Think about your audience and what they care about, and tailor your message to them. It's not unloading everything you know at once, it's thinking about what you want to say and how you can say it to match your listeners' expectations. This reframe is powerful because it helps you communicate more proactively versus reactively. It gets you thinking about how you can logically structure your delivery so it lands with impact. It also challenges you to step out of your own head so that you're not just staying silent and hoping for the best. You're thinking about how you can capture your audience's attention. To implement this reframe, consider these questions before your next meeting:

- Who is going to be there?
- What do they care about?
- How can I align my points with what motivates them?

Here's an example: Let's say you're about to give a presentation to your team about a project you're working on. The objective of that meeting is to get them to understand how the project will impact them, its benefits, and how it'll make their job easier—things you know they care about. However, if you are making the same presentation, but this time to senior leaders, instead of talking about the exact same points in the exact same way, you should ask yourself, "What do these senior leaders care about, and how can I align my points with what motivates them?" The answer might now revolve around resource allocation, the time needed to get the project done, and the return on investment—things you know leadership tends to prioritize.

In the communication world, this is called the communication accommodation theory, and it is what differentiates being just a talker from being an effective speaker. The theory suggests that when we keep our audience in mind and adjust our message to them, it enhances mutual understanding and achieves better engagement. Here's another example of tailoring our message to what our audience cares about: If a person likes to receive information in a straightforward and simple way, adding any embellishments, like background information, can dilute the impact of that message. On the flip side, if someone wants context, data, and explanations and we give them only high-level talking points, they may feel like we didn't give them enough information to make a good decision.

Further illustrating the importance of thinking about our audience and tailoring our speaking to them, research has shown that people judge others based on their communication style much more than how they control a situation. For example, a study looked at students' perceptions of their teachers and found that if the teacher used a favored communication style, students perceived the quality of that teaching to be higher, because they had a positive impression of how the teacher spoke.

At this point, you may be thinking, what if you haven't fleshed out your idea yet? Should you remain quiet and keep your thoughts to yourself? For those of us raised in a Quiet Culture, it's easy to default to staying silent, because researching and processing our ideas fully before sharing them comes naturally. At baseline, it's important to note that we should not nod our head in agreement if we don't agree with others and their ideas, because when we do, we are not actually engaging at all. We are compromising ourselves for the sake of others. Instead, we should trust that if we don't yet have our ideas or talking points fully solidified, we can still add our thoughts to the conversation, even if it's just our initial impressions—because just having our voice heard is oftentimes half the battle to getting noticed.

Now, there is an element of psychological safety that is necessary for people to feel safe chiming in at work, so I don't discount the difficulty of engaging if that safety isn't there. But it is worth noting that sometimes the belief in ourselves and our ideas, and how they can benefit others, can be the catalyst for how we engage with others and make ourselves heard. Because the real question isn't whether we should or should not proactively communicate, it's how can we structure our message so it resonates with the person we're talking to. I will share more communication tactics in part 3, but in the meantime, adding our thoughts and ideas and tailoring them to what our audience cares about can give us the visibility needed to be noticed the way we want to be.

Back to Chung's story and the communication friction she was experiencing with her boss. Chung knew it needed to be addressed, so she found a good time to bring it up. What her boss said opened her eyes to the root of their problem. It came down to their mismatched communication styles. Chung said her own preference for talking about her work was to take loads of information and paint a vivid picture with context and details. But what her manager wanted was for that information to be distilled and centralized into simple points.

Her manager put it this way: "You're a multiple input to multiple output [person], and I am a single input to a single output [person]."

Chung said this was a light bulb moment. Understanding whom she was speaking with and then doing the work to tailor her delivery to the preference of her listener made engaging more seamless. "Suddenly my analytical brain realized, 'Oh, it's not personal. I just have to change how I talk to her and how I draft things.' It changed our relationship one hundred percent."

Whether you feel firmly planted in your Quiet Culture approach or you veer more toward the middle when speaking, remember that an effective communicator is neither quiet nor loud. It is someone who can think about their audience, tailor their message to them, and showcase their ideas so the message lands with intent. This brings us to the second point: how we spend our time.

SPEND TIME: HOW WE PREFER TO WORK

CULTURAL REFRAME

Maximize every opportunity

It was the beginning of a new workweek. Reporters and producers were filing into our morning editorial meeting at the NBC News 4 station in Reno, Nevada, ready to kick off the day. I beelined to the first open seat, sat down, and pulled out my phone. With five minutes to spare, I googled "top stories" and started scrolling through the daily news. However, all around me, I could hear my colleagues catching up and bantering.

"Matt, how was your weekend?" Carrie called from across the room.

"Hey Karen, I checked out that restaurant you talked about," said another.

For a full five minutes, the room was bustling and lively—a mark of a Loud Culture environment. But I was sitting there with my eyes glued to the phone, quietly working. No one was engaging with me, and I wasn't engaging with them. Instead, as someone raised in a Quiet Culture, I was doing what had been ingrained in me: spending time working, down to the last minute, to demonstrate that I was a hard worker. But something about this wasn't right.

For those of us who grew up in a Quiet Culture, values such as being disciplined, putting in the hours, and working hard resonate deeply. I remember my parents instilled in me the importance of developing a strong work ethic. They reiterated how *they* worked hard by putting in the long hours, working overtime, and sacrificing their own pleasures, because time spent was about doing what they were told to do at work. So they told us kids to embody the same behaviors: don't "waste time," "follow instructions," and "always work hard." As a child, this specifically translated into extracurricular activities, such as after-school tutoring, weekend classes, and math lessons, among many other enrichment activities. As painful as it was to be shuttled from activity to activity, the promise was that as long as we followed this path and worked hard, we would eventually be rewarded for it too.

Fast-forward to adulthood and the working world, and it becomes clear that while time spent working hard matters, it's not the only path to success, and it's *not* always rewarded. Instead, what is rewarded is the time spent building rapport and strengthening relationships. It's also about building visibility and influence internally and externally. These soft skills and more people-related activities, while not always producing immediate, definable results, can lead to more opportunities, introductions, and closing the deal down the line. For example, here is a career tip currently being shared among management consultants across the country today: Apart from meeting the necessary qualifications and technical skills of the job, aspiring consultants are told to prioritize passing the "airport test," which is determining whether someone would want to spend time with them at an airport. Albeit subjective, it highlights how important building connections and engaging with people is, an often unspoken rule of a Loud Culture workplace.

Sitting in that editorial meeting that fateful Monday, I realized that working down to the last minute was hurting me more than it was helping me. Although I was indeed showing I was "a hard worker" and taking the job seriously, I was also just a part of the background, utterly unmemorable, because people were not getting to know *me*. It was in this moment that I knew I had to rethink how I showed up and spent my time at work.

So the Cultural Reframe for Spend Time is: Maximize every opportunity. At first glance, this reframe may seem like it is about being overt. However, what "Maximize every opportunity" means is thinking about the big picture and ensuring we are making the most of every project we're assigned to. I often think back to the business of running a family restaurant: What the restaurant cooks is only one part of an entire dining experience. Meaning, if the restaurant wants to make the best possible impression, they can't just think about the dishes they're cooking behind the scenes; they have to also think about every touch point they have with the customer, such as the food presentation, staff etiquette, and even their communications. Similarly, we can maximize every opportunity at work by ensuring we're not just quietly working behind the scenes, but are also looking for touch points with our team so they can *see* the impact our work has.

For instance, if our job is to build financial models for forecasting, budgeting, and decision-making, how can we let others know what we're doing as we're doing it? It doesn't have to be a long-winded exchange. It can be a simple FYI. Or if we discover something that made us say "wow" as we were conducting our research, can we share it with others as a heads-up, or as a way to tease what we have coming up? Doing so is neither forceful nor inauthentic, it is proactive.

Another powerful attribute of this Cultural Reframe is when we are assigned to do work we don't want to do or we think is a "waste of time," instead of dwelling or sulking, we can take an ownership mentality and brainstorm ways to paint ourselves in the best possible light while doing the work.

Here's an example of taking the work we're given and building visibility around it. Let's say you have been tasked with the not-so-exciting project of organizing a team's Excel spreadsheet so it reads more easily. While you know it's going to take hours and it is not work you particularly enjoy doing, by reframing your approach to maximize every opportunity, you can now find ways to talk about the work and let people know what's going on as you're doing it. This includes giving your manager a quick update, or even shooting a five-minute demo video at the end of the project so that you can teach others how they can best utilize this new spreadsheet. You can even treat the video as a conversation starter with other cross-functional teams by sharing how this is something they can consider doing as well. The point is to think about the work—the big projects and the small projects—and use it as a catalyst to expand your visibility and influence, because *that* is time well spent.

Furthermore, by creating more touch points, we can increase what psychologists call our "halo effect." This is the opinion people have of us in one area that is based on their impressions from another area. For instance, when we do good work on one project, that positive impression puts us in good standing for other work and for other projects going forward, effectively compounding the positive influence we have. Because here's the truth: when people know us and like us, they are more willing to bat for us when other opportunities arise. *That* is a great way to maximize every opportunity.

Now let's talk about the third point: how we celebrate our achievements.

HANDLE WINS: HOW WE CELEBRATE OUR ACHIEVEMENTS

CULTURAL REFRAME

Share how your work
benefits the greater good

A few months into working at the NBC station in Reno, I received a tip I couldn't stop thinking about. I got word a convicted sex offender was living in a nursing home and had sexually assaulted an elderly resident there. Worse, it wasn't the first time this person had harmed a fellow resident.

How could this have happened not once, but twice? Were there any precautions put in place the first time? If so, how could this have happened again? Anger rushed through me as the questions flooded my mind. I was desperate to do the story because I knew that if done right, it could lead to changes that would protect other vulnerable residents in nursing homes across the state. So the investigative work began.

Over a span of several weeks, I logged hours of phone conversations and in-person interviews with the victim's family. I reached out to the nursing facility multiple times, and to the sex offender's family to get their side of the story. I called lawmakers and attorneys and spent hours at the county records office to source and corroborate critical information. I also spent time furiously searching the internet to glean insight that would make the story stronger. I was doing this on top of the work I needed to do every day, but I didn't mind. I was committed to finding all the answers to highlight what happened.

During this period, I had mentioned to my manager I was pursuing this story on the side. He was thrilled, because we were the only news station investigating it. Every few days, he would ask how things were going, but I didn't divulge too much information because I didn't feel the story was ready. I would simply say, "It's coming along," and minimize the hours worked.

As I neared the end of the research, I finally discovered the hook to the story. According to Nevada law, nursing homes weren't required to be informed that a resident was a registered sex offender unless they were a tier III, the most serious type of offender. In this case, the suspect was a tier II. Therein was the answer the victim's family was looking for. They could now use this critical piece of information to lobby for change and demand that nursing homes around the state be notified of this information and disclose it to residents and their families. Once I compiled the research and findings, I met with my manager to show the final piece. He gave it a resounding stamp of approval.

"Hey—great job with the story!" my boss said.

Instinctively, I smiled and immediately downplayed my efforts. "Thanks, it was no big deal."

As I returned to my desk, a mental dialogue started running through my head. Why did I respond with "It was no big deal" when in fact it was a big deal? Why did I reduce my accomplishment when it had taken a lot of effort? I had poured my heart into researching the story, sacrificing my free time to make sure I didn't miss a thing. Why did I diminish the work? In fact, this would've been the perfect time to talk about leading bigger projects, now that I had demonstrated my willingness to go above and beyond. But because of my inability to showcase my achievement, my boss couldn't see that I was capable of more.

As frustrating as it was to feel this sense of friction, deep down I knew exactly why I was feeling it. Because I was raised with Quiet Culture values, it was not in my nature to talk about my work in such an overt way. I had always been told to stay humble, not boast, and to keep accomplishments to myself. In fact, I was never really taught *how* to accept praise and compliments gracefully and comfortably. Instead, what I was told was to deny the compliment as a way of showing modesty. But now, in a Loud Culture workplace, because I diminished my own accomplishments, I muted them in the process too.

For many of us raised in a Quiet Culture, we not only feel awkward about praise and compliments, we prefer to have our work speak for itself, rather than draw attention to it. We think or hope that if we do good work, people will just notice it, and we won't have to showcase our wins. We also shy away from saying too much because we don't want others to feel like we think we are better than them. Or, perhaps more perniciously, we downplay our efforts because we think maybe what we accomplished was just luck.

How we handle wins is arguably one of the harder values to reframe because how we talk about ourselves is a reflection of how we truly feel. If we don't think we deserve the win or praise, we won't talk about it. If we feel like our work isn't up to par, we won't focus on what we did right. Instead, we will just think about what we missed. It is difficult to encourage people who value humbleness to self-promote. Of course, we don't want to discount the importance of humility, which we know can lead to better interpersonal relationships, increased trust, and enhanced group cohesion. But the problem with diminishing our contributions is that it mutes the work we do, including what others may think we are capable of. Reframing how we handle wins, therefore, is important so we can get the recognition we deserve.

So the Cultural Reframe for Handle Wins is: Share how our work benefits the greater good. This means demonstrating how our work has helped an individual, the team, and even the business. The recognition can be short and sweet, including in one-on-one check-ins or via email, but the key is to communicate so others can see the *benefit* of our efforts. Examples of benefits can be streamlining, clarifying, organizing, or advancing an initiative. In fact, research has found that when individuals frame their achievements in terms of the greater good, it induces in others a state of moral elevation. For instance, when we see someone do something helpful, we will be more compelled to help others too. In other words, highlighting the benefits of our work can foster positive organizational outcomes and cooperation. Furthermore, sharing how our work contributes to the greater good can create a sense of cohesion and harmony that shows we're team players and we're in it together—a true win-win situation. So remember, being humble is not about thinking less of ourselves; it's thinking about ourselves in the context of how we're helping others.

Next, let's talk about how we manage conflict.

MANAGE CONFLICT: HOW WE HANDLE TRICKY SITUATIONS

CULTURAL REFRAME

Focus on the dynamics at play

It was a crisp day in the Bay Area, yet Cheryl Cheng was feeling uncomfortably warm. Cheng is the founder and CEO of Vive Collective, a company that builds, funds, and scales next-generation digital health companies in Palo Alto, California.

But early in her career, when she was working for a large consumer products brand, she had to navigate shutting down a failing project.

"It was one of the hardest things I ever had to do," Cheng said. "I had to kill a project because the numbers just weren't there."

For weeks, she brainstormed how she would deliver the tricky news to her senior leadership team. The negative news would of course shake up the team's plan, but it would also cause a lot of anger and disruption. Furthermore, saying something this extreme could shatter her credibility, because she could be seen as dropping the ball. She had to tread carefully; she did not want to rock the boat.

For those of us raised in a Quiet Culture, when things don't go according to plan, we may go into a fight-or-flight mode, and our instinct is flight. We avoid the situation, because we find conflict incredibly uncomfortable. We hate the tension, the awkward silence, the feeling that we're in trouble or that we're making other people feel like they're in trouble. So we avoid confrontation, acquiesce, or even hide. Sometimes, we may even keep our head down and grind away, hoping the problem will resolve itself. But the reality is, this way of thinking is not productive for managing tough situations, especially when our reputation is on the line. When we're working in a Loud Culture, our colleagues may see our desire to dodge tough conversations as avoidant or not transparent, because they approach tricky situations by "talking it out" and "getting it all on the table." They want direct and clear dialogue, and while it may not always be comfortable for them, they know it's a means to an end.

So the Cultural Reframe for Manage Conflict is: Focus on the dynamics at play. This means recognizing that conflicts do not occur in a vacuum, and many factors are always at play. While our instinct may be to avoid tough situations, instead, we need to pivot to focus on *context*. This approach is called transformative mediation, which describes focusing on understanding who is involved, how to handle the situation, and how to minimize damage. In other words, we need to switch our mentality from simply running and hiding to considering all people, all perspectives, and all circumstances, because work is a melding of people and ideas, and things are better solved together.

To cement this reframe, we can ask ourselves a few questions to get us back on track when things don't go as planned. This will give us a better understanding of the dynamics at play, including the who, what, when, and where in our environment. The questions are:

- Who needs to know so no one is surprised?
- What can we say to ensure everyone feels they're in the loop and not blindsided?
- When is the appropriate time to say something so it's best received?
- Where should this conversation take place?

Answering these questions will help us address uncomfortable situations with honesty and clarity. The beauty of this Cultural Reframe is that it's neither quiet nor loud. It is subtle yet powerful.

For Cheng, shutting down that large initiative was not going to be easy, because so much time and money had already been spent on the project. But one thing was clear: she couldn't just hide behind her desk for the sake of peace. So, Cheng leaned in to this Cultural Reframe by studying the dynamics at play, looking at who was involved, and crafting what she could say so she wouldn't catch people off guard. She calculated the best time to share the information and decided she would not dump all the bad news at once. Because if she did, it would cause a disastrous chain reaction, with people pointing fingers and assigning blame.

"If I had communicated on week one that we were going to kill the project, I would have lost an incredible amount of credibility, because they would have said, 'You're jumping the gun,'" Cheng said.

So, over time, she unveiled new details and metrics to get her senior leaders to see the reality of the situation. In essence, she was priming them, which is what psychologists say is influencing people to think or feel a certain way by exposing them to specific bits of information over time. In her meetings, Cheng said she asked carefully prepared questions to prompt her team to think that hitting the goal was actually much harder to do. She didn't blurt out, "Let's kill the project." Instead, she let them come to that conclusion themselves.

"I know what I ultimately want to communicate; I just need to get you there at the right time so it's not a shock," she said.

Some may see Cheng's method as too slow, but it's a strategic marriage of having a thoughtful approach and delivering it with tact. It's neither hiding nor causing violent waves. It is thinking about the who, what, when, and where, and having a plan in place.

"If you don't communicate it in the right cadence or time, you lose a tremendous amount of credibility because [others] feel like you haven't done the work," Cheng said.

The truth is, this reframe is easier to practice when we have the time to think about what we want to do. But sometimes conflict and tricky conversations happen suddenly. Our manager will pull us into a meeting and ask a pointed question about why things aren't going as planned. Hiding is not an option, and running through the checklist of the dynamics at play may not be feasible. So if this happens, it's important not to deflect or blame. Instead, consider how we can communicate what we know and explain our reasoning. Adding context can soften the blow. The key is to clue others in to what's going on and what has happened, because conflict is often made much worse when people are shocked and caught off guard. In the working world, people don't like being surprised because it can make them look unprepared. So don't shy away from providing context, managing people's expectations, and being honest as ways to manage tough situations.

THE CULTURAL REFRAMES

ENGAGE OTHERS	SPEND TIME	HANDLE WINS	MANAGE CONFLICT
Tailor your message to your audience	Maximize every opportunity	Share how your work benefits the greater good	Focus on the dynamics at play

SHIFTING HOW WE show up in the workplace isn't about eliminating what we know and love from the values we were raised with. It's about reframing how we apply our Quiet Culture approach in a Loud Culture world so it better serves us. Everything covered in this chapter is meant to broaden, enhance, and armor the person we are with the mindset and tools to get noticed for all the right reasons. But I'd be remiss if I didn't acknowledge that there is still an uphill battle to climb for many of us Quiet Culture individuals to be more visible. It is the Quiet Culture bias, including the things we tell ourselves, that we will cover next.

Reframing
Black-and-White Thinking

Casey Wen had just started working at a private equity firm in New York City when she began to feel conflicted about how to show up and speak up in meetings. Growing up in Singapore, she'd embodied many of the values found in a Quiet Culture, including working hard, listening to her seniors, and staying humble.

"I grew up with a lot of fear about people's perception of me," Casey admitted. "This has prevented me from thinking and reasoning properly, particularly in high-stress situations."

Just a few months into her new role, Casey saw that her colleagues, many of whom were from a Loud Culture, communicated directly, loudly, and even abrasively. While this was different from what she was used to, she took note that in order to succeed, she needed to be just like them to be noticed too.

"I was in a meeting last week and I felt one of my colleagues—who is also on my level—kept talking over me," Casey explained. "I was afraid that if I let her keep dominating, she would hog up all the airtime and I would be seen as more inexperienced. So, I made sure to keep talking. It was incredibly uncomfortable."

Casey was responding to the situation *not* in a way that came naturally to her, but in a way she thought she needed to. But because it was not in her nature to be loud, it felt uncomfortable, awkward, and psychologically taxing.

Once Casey and I started working together, I knew what she needed help with: reframing how to Engage Others and Manage Conflict. We worked on having her rethink her approach of how she handled tricky situations, such as when her colleague would talk over her in meetings. Instead of seeing it as "me versus them," or "they win, I lose," she needed to step back and think about the dynamics at play. For example, she should consider context, use inclusive language, and work on how she could better chime in. We also discussed how she could address the tense dynamic in a one-on-one conversation, instead of exerting herself in a forced way in front of her entire team.

In addition, while it was great that she was voicing her thoughts frequently in meetings, she needed to rethink that talking in a domineering way was the *only* way to get her point across, like it was a black-or-white choice. Instead, she needed to look at her Engage Others reframe and ask: What is the purpose of the meeting? Who is in the meeting? How can I structure my message to the things people care about so they listen? Doing this would ensure she spoke with quality content, not quantity of content. Because it was not about how loud she spoke, it was how tailored her speaking could be. Over a span of several weeks, this new mindset and approach started to click.

"I'd been so focused on getting people to hear and notice me that I neglected to think about the dynamics. I needed to step back, find the middle ground, and think more about others, *not* just about defending myself or my ideas," she said.

Just like Casey, sometimes when we enter a Loud Culture workplace, we can veer too far into thinking we must change ourselves to fit in. But the key is to keep our Cultural Reframes in mind, so we can speak up and show up in a way that feels right. Casey discovered it wasn't about changing her Quiet Culture traits; it was about focusing on her Cultural Reframes to give her the tools to be heard and seen.

WORD TO THE WISE

 Black-and-white thinking is feeling like there is only one solution to a problem. It's thinking we must change ourselves and be loud in order to succeed. But the truth is, our Cultural Reframes are a balanced way of approaching the Loud Culture workplace, without complete acculturation.

So how can you identify which Cultural Reframe(s) to focus on? One way is to pay attention to your physical sensations when something uncomfortable happens at work. For example, does your stomach turn when you want to say something in a meeting? This might be a sign to focus on Engage Others. Or does your heart start racing when someone compliments and praises you at work? Maybe look into how you Handle Wins. Listening to your body is a great place to start, and it will give you a sense of which Cultural Reframes to work on first.

THE BOTTOM LINE

- Finding success and building visibility in the workplace do not require us to behave loudly if we have quiet traits.

- Reframing our Quiet Culture values can help us expand how we work in a Loud Culture without complete acculturation.

- The Cultural Reframe for how we **Engage Others** is to tailor our message to what our audience cares about.

- The Cultural Reframe for how we **Spend Time** is to maximize every opportunity.

- The Cultural Reframe for how we **Handle Wins** is to share how our work benefits the greater good.

- The Cultural Reframe for how we **Manage Conflict** is to focus on the dynamics at play.

CHAPTER 3

OVERCOMING THE QUIET CULTURE BIAS

Perception and what we tell ourselves

The moment I realized I had been raised with Quiet Culture values but was operating in a Loud Culture workplace was the beginning of a yearslong journey to finding more workplace clarity and confidence. I created the Cultural Reframes and applied them to how I engaged with others, spent time, handled wins, and managed conflict, and I *intentionally* practiced them at work. More important, I began to *feel* the difference. I was no longer sitting in meetings ruminating about and questioning people's perceptions of me. I could now better read the room and offer value. Thoughts of "Should I speak up?" and "Should I showcase my work?" were now reframed as "How can I?"

As you begin to think about and apply your Cultural Reframes at work, you will discover they are strategic ways of approaching the workplace that are neither quiet nor loud. They take what can often be frustrating encounters, in which we don't know what to do or what to say, and we create a new path forward. But the truth is, it will take effort. These are new approaches, after all. Sometimes it will feel easier to speak up in meetings and tailor our message to what our audience cares about, while other times, it will feel easier to just default to staying silent. Thinking through and applying these Cultural Reframes will be an ongoing practice, because you will find that despite thinking about your audience, maximizing every opportunity, showcasing your work, and focusing on the dynamics at play, the ride to being noticed exactly the way you want to be will still be bumpy. From time to time, you will even see opportunities pass you by, and you might wonder if the Cultural Reframes really work. The answer is yes, but the reality is, we are facing a Quiet Culture bias.

The Quiet Culture bias is the perception that because we may have a more quiet disposition, we are somehow meek or even weak. Because we prefer to work hard and keep our heads down, we are only good workers, not leaders. Because we don't talk about our achievements as much as others, we probably don't have any. And because we avoid conflict, we can't handle tough conversations and manage others. Worse yet, when we do speak up, we may even face backlash, because it's not how others expect us to act. If we add a racial or ethnic consideration to our Quiet Culture behavior, the cultural dissonance is compounded.

In fact, we know women and people of color experience more instances of being unseen, unacknowledged, and forgotten at work. Researchers say there are four kinds of intersectional invisibility: erasure, homogenization, exoticization, and whitening. Erasure is the most literal in that we are unheard or invisible. Homogenization is being treated like a homogeneous, interchangeable member of an out-group. Exoticization is being reduced to foreign objects of fascination and fetishization. And whitening is being complimented because we have similarities to white people, or we have our racial and ethnic identities and our cultural backgrounds discounted or ignored.

Personally, as an Asian woman whose values align with those found in a Quiet Culture, I have found myself sitting in meetings where I will say what's on my mind, but then that suggestion will be treated like it was never made, vanishing into thin air.

Recently, I had an experience that perfectly exemplifies the biases we can often face. Despite feeling fairly confident navigating a Loud Culture, as well as having spent years applying my Cultural Reframes in the workplace, I felt profoundly disappointed after a lunch meeting with an executive. I was there to discuss acquiring a board seat, but within just ten minutes of sitting down, this executive had one agenda: to talk about his fascination with Asian culture and my upbringing, not the business at hand.

"Let me guess—was obeying your parents a hallmark of your childhood? Did you have zero say in your career aspirations, like you could only be a doctor or lawyer?" he asked with an air of amusement.

"Growing up, did you do any of these things: drink hot water at restaurants, reuse old grocery bags as garbage bags, or take off your shoes at home?" he continued.

Stunned at where he was taking this meeting, I politely redirected the conversation to the topic at hand. But this executive couldn't be swayed. I realized I was no longer sitting in a meeting talking about what I could bring to the table; I was sitting in a meeting talking about being a dutiful Asian girl. Needless to say, it was extremely disappointing, and I left the meeting early. As I walked out, I felt a sense of dismay. In my heart, I knew this behavior was beyond a Quiet Culture bias; it was just bias.

In the days after this lunch meeting, I couldn't help but wonder if I was fighting a losing battle. I wondered if, as a double minority—a woman and a person of color—with the added layer of coming from a Quiet Culture, I was always going to be perceived as less than, a follower, a worker unworthy of leadership roles. Was I going to have to fight all the time just to be recognized, valued, and seen?

There is no question that identifying with a certain ethnic group can add a layer of complexity to the Quiet Culture bias. Sometimes it will feel easier to just scream defeat and retreat to our Quiet Culture behaviors. But the reality is, if we let this narrative seed itself in our minds, we won't be able to expand and challenge ourselves in new ways. Keeping ourselves hidden and silent maintains the power structure of those who already have no problem being heard and seen. So if our workplace is a Loud Culture and we don't push ourselves to grow beyond the behaviors of what we know, we will become utterly invisible, falling further behind in opportunity.

THE COURAGE TO TRY

For those of us raised with Quiet Culture values, one of our greatest strengths is our ability to internalize and process things thoroughly. In a fast-paced world, our ability to listen, observe, and get things done is a tremendous asset. We are resourceful and great at solving problems, which we often can do on our own. However, our ability to go at it alone can sometimes cause us to *stay* alone. Or worse yet, we let things be, because we don't want to inconvenience others. For example, at work, if we want to join a high-visibility project, we will ask for it once, get told no, and then assume that as long as we tried, that's all that matters. There is indeed peace in being content with how things fall into place, but if we see something we really want, we have to find the courage to try and try again.

This is where I want to talk about overcoming the *internal* Quiet Culture bias, specifically the things we tell ourselves. Earlier, I talked about the *external* Quiet Culture bias, which is how others can perceive our quieter disposition as weak. But just as robustly, the Quiet Culture bias can come from the voice in our head. For example, there might be a narrative in our mind saying, "I don't want to fail," or "I don't want to look silly," so we stay within the confines of what we know. Some of us may even be pulled into the notion of "saving face," in which doing something out of our comfort zone can put us in the vulnerable position of feeling embarrassed, especially if things don't work out.

The problem with believing our own Quiet Culture bias is that it prevents us from reaching our fullest potential. When we let anxiety, fear of humiliation, or fear of judgment take over, we cut ourselves off from the visibility we need to be recognized at work. What we should do instead is gift ourselves the most selfless offering we can: be one less critic in a world full of critics. We know that when we go against the grain, or step into something new or uncomfortable, it will feel scary. But we have to replace our limiting thoughts with more self-compassionate ones. We have to believe that what we're doing matters, because it absolutely does. So even if we don't have all the answers, foolproof research, or even English as our first language, know that the richness of our work experience *is* our ability to share and celebrate it with other people.

To help us overcome our internal Quiet Culture bias, I've developed my own pragmatic system to check and recheck myself whenever I find that I'm doubting my abilities or questioning how I should show up at work. Because as humans, it's not unusual for us to want to avoid feelings of uncertainty, especially when our reputation is on the line. We stick to what feels safe. Researchers call this the permanence effect, and it is the tendency for us to stick to our beliefs and not change our minds about them. So to combat any limiting beliefs and to get us feeling comfortable putting ourselves out there, I crafted the Journalist's Approach as a way of challenging my own Quiet

Culture bias and rethinking these beliefs. This approach was inspired by my industry, where, as journalists, we are trained to see the world through the lens of positive skepticism. We listen to what people say, but we also question the validity of it before we internalize it. The Journalist's Approach is applicable in the journalism world, but it is also effective for combating any beliefs that might hold us back.

We can apply this approach by replacing our "I don't . . ." statements with "How do I know . . . ?" Then, we challenge ourselves to think of a few reasons why we think we *can't* do something or why something bad *will* happen if we do.

QUIET CULTURE BIAS	THE JOURNALIST'S APPROACH
• I don't think I can do it. • I don't want to look silly. • I don't want to fail. • I don't want to be taken advantage of. • I don't think they'll care.	• How do I know I can't do it? • How do I know I will look silly? • How do I know I will fail? • How do I know I will be taken advantage of? • How do I know they won't care?

If we look at the internal Quiet Culture bias sentences on the left, we can see that these phrases, when posed as statements, can form a very narrow interpretation of what we're actually capable of. The Journalist's Approach helps us create a space where we can keep things open to interpretation, thereby allowing unexpected outcomes to blossom. If we can't say for certain that we can't do something or that something bad will happen, then we shouldn't take our Quiet Culture bias at face value. Instead, we should trust ourselves, put ourselves out there, and give it our best shot. This is cognitive reframing at work, and it can increase our willingness to try new things because *that* is when the most unexpected opportunities start to open up.

Naming the Limiting Beliefs

When I first jumped on a call with Kathy Tu, I was unsure where the meeting was going. Kathy had reached out for communications help, but from the looks of it, she seemed to be communicating just fine. She had a bright, sunny demeanor, and her speaking was clear and engaging. Her nonverbal communication skills, such as smiling and using hand gestures, were also on point.

Then she said it: "My problem is I always assume the worst."

I asked her to elaborate.

"If my boss gives me constructive feedback, my mind goes racing. I'm sure I did something totally wrong, or I pissed off a client. I also start talking really fast," she said.

What she was experiencing is what some of us in the communications world call Racing Brain syndrome. For many people, when we get feedback, our brain assumes the worst. For example, we think our manager is going to lose respect for us, we're going to get called in to HR, or worse, we're going to get fired. Because we were caught off guard and now feel nervous, we start hurling words, getting defensive, and talking in circles. For those of us raised in a Quiet Culture, this is a common way of responding to conflict. The smallest pieces of feedback can be magnified in our minds.

Kathy knew much of the constructive feedback was never actually that bad and that she wasn't going to get fired, but she wanted to get a grip on how she responded to it. She wanted help reframing her response so she could go from debilitated to taking action. So, we decided to label her negative self-talk. I started the process with an unexpected question.

"What is your least favorite vegetable?" I asked.

"Celery?" Kathy responded, seeming confused.

"Great, let's label your negative self-talk the word *celery*," I said. "When you see yourself going down this dark rabbit hole of negative self-talk, say to yourself, 'Celery, this is too much. Stop!'"

Kathy laughed. It was silly, but she got the point.

Labeling, if used consciously, is a cognitive technique that can help us identify negative thoughts when they arise so we can acknowledge they're happening. In Kathy's case, by labeling her negative self-talk "celery," she could address it directly in her mind, as if it were a tangible object she could envision. Plus, creating this distinction between her and the thought gave her brain a chance to switch its thinking.

Similarly, just as much as we can recognize and label negative self-talk, we can also label positive self-talk as a way to redirect our thinking.

"What's your favorite vegetable?" I then asked.

"Mushrooms," Kathy responded.

"Great—let's label the positive self-talk 'mushroom.' The mushroom is the voice that says, 'Wait a minute, it's not the end of the world. Calm down, take a breath. It's OK.' In a panicky moment, you can say to yourself, 'Let's have the mushroom get us back on track!'"

As Kathy and I reflected on this approach, she pulled out two sticky notes and wrote "Celery" on one paper and "Mushroom" on the other. She taped both notes to her desk and smiled. "Now that I can see them, I will always remember them!"

These words, as silly as they are, can serve as a visual reminder of what we tell ourselves and what we choose to believe. When our internal Quiet Culture bias gets too loud, we can remember that there are indeed two voices in our head, and we have the power to listen to the one that helps us the most.

WORD TO THE WISE

 Think back to a situation in which you found yourself frozen in fear or going down a rabbit hole of negative, limiting thoughts. What were those thoughts telling you? Did you automatically assume the worst? A good indication of when this is happening is going back to the body and feeling the physical sensations— heart pounding, stomach churning, nausea, and so on.

If you notice you're being particularly hard on yourself for more than five minutes, take a breath, acknowledge that it's just negative self-talk, and label it. Then ask yourself, "How do I know this to be true, and what can I do now?"

OUR BEST CHEERLEADER

For some of us, overcoming the Quiet Culture bias is a choice, because we want to grow personally and professionally; for others, stepping outside our comfort zone is a matter of survival. Earlier in this book, I shared how my family immigrated to the US from Taiwan, and how they banded together to open a family restaurant called Peach Garden. My mom, the youngest of eight children, worked as a waitress until she had me and my brother. Then, for more than two decades, she assumed the role of homemaker and filled her days with the responsibilities of creating a peaceful home and caring for her family. She did this because she wanted to ensure we were getting support at home, and perhaps more important, to ensure we weren't getting in trouble! For her, this predictable pace meshed well with her Quiet Culture values of just doing what was asked, not creating waves, and maintaining a harmonious environment.

However, everything changed as soon as I graduated from college. My parents got divorced, and my mom found herself needing to go back to work. The road to integrate herself into the working world was steep. The restaurant our family once owned had been sold. She had to start again from the bottom— learning how to use new technology, navigate office politics, and communicate effectively with colleagues in a workplace where English was the dominant language. As my mom navigated a Loud Culture work environment, she felt the raw vulnerability of being an immigrant once again—a foreigner unsure of how to navigate even the basics. But instead of entering a new country, she was now experiencing this feeling at work. She eventually found a job as a sales associate for the Japanese beauty brand Shiseido.

"There was no other choice but to keep trying," my mom said as she reflected on those early days.

She said there were difficult times when she wasn't sure if she could last. There were loud coworkers who brazenly took advantage of her naivete, and hostile customers who were downright mean. As a result, thoughts like *I don't think I can do this* and *I don't think I am cut out for this* filled her mind, especially at the end of the day.

"Learning new technology was incredibly hard. Using the right English took practice too," she said. "But here's the thing— I never allowed myself to think I couldn't do it for too long."

My mom said that despite coming from a Quiet Culture— which influenced how she interacted with others—she realized there was no other way but to reframe how she approached work. She needed a job, and she needed the help of others. Instead of dwelling on how foreign everything seemed, she focused on what she could control by rewiring any limiting beliefs she had. She then thought about engaging with her team by conceptualizing how they could pair products so that, as a group, they could increase sales together. She ensured she maximized every opportunity by reaching out to customers to make them feel special, as if they were getting an exclusive notice about a specific product or launch, so she could stay top of mind. She also gave regular shout-outs to people on her team so that when she called out her own wins, it didn't feel one-sided. And if there ever was conflict, she did not hide, but thought about who needed to know and what the plan of action was, so there was honesty and transparency. She worked in exactly the way this book recommends: smart, not loud.

"I always wrote things down so I would never forget. I made good friends with others who were patient and nice to me, and I made sure to always highlight how great *we* were doing as a team. Every day, it got better."

In just a few years, the way my mom carried herself in a Loud Culture workplace became truly remarkable. Her tendency to keep quiet, keep her head down, and avoid the spotlight was transformed into a new way of working and showing up. She didn't throw away her Quiet Culture; instead, she reframed her values so she could *thrive* in a Loud Culture. She went from being a reserved homemaker to being a successful and well-liked employee. Just a few years into her role, she was promoted to manager and was one of the highest-performing employees in the entire department store, where she raked in four hundred thousand dollars of cosmetics sales in one year.

Her own contact list of clients had a recurring purchase order of 37 percent—way above her counter's average. Not bad for a small beauty counter in suburbia headed by a former stay-at-home mom in her fifties.

I share this story because my mom's ability to make such a drastic transformation was the result of what she allowed herself to think. She recognized she needed to mold herself not only because it was necessary but also because it was empowering to embody a new way of approaching the workplace. While navigating this new construct, she also unlocked a side of herself she had never seen. It was a kind of self-confidence and self-assurance that she attributed to having a growth mindset.

"You have to be your own best cheerleader, because if not you, who else?" she said.

KEEP IT GOING

When we think about reframing how we engage others, spend time at work, handle wins, and manage conflict, we need to consider the Quiet Culture bias too. This comes from how people choose to see us, as well as what we tell ourselves, both of which can shape our sense of self. Shifting people's perceptions of us will take time, but we can control how we approach the workplace every day. For example, acknowledging that we can be our own harshest critic can minimize the negative self-talk we do. Or that the pain, friction, and awkward conversations we experience are actually part of putting ourselves out there. In other words, it's telling ourselves that we need to stop focusing on saving face, and start showing face. As long as we continue to challenge ourselves, feel hopeful about our progress, and reflect from time to time, we will begin to be noticed the way we want to be.

SO FAR, WE'VE SPENT time discussing the two constructs of Quiet Culture and Loud Culture and how the way we were raised reinforces certain behaviors. Then when we enter the working world, we feel a sense of culture shock, because what we were taught contrasts with what's now expected of us. The key, though, isn't to jump ship and try to adopt Loud Culture traits if that's not who we are. Instead, it's to position ourselves to get noticed for the right reasons. This is where the Cultural Reframes come into play. These reframes provide a new way of thinking about our behavior that doesn't require us to be only quiet or only loud.

With this mindset in place, our next step is to figure out what to do. And that's where the Quiet Capital Framework, which we'll discuss in part 2, comes in.

THE BOTTOM LINE

- The Quiet Culture bias is the perception that because someone has a quiet disposition, they are meek or weak.

- This bias can come from both what people think of us and what we say to ourselves.

- Overcoming the Quiet Culture bias requires self-compassion and going from saving face to showing face.

- Labeling our negative thoughts is a cognitive technique that can help us identify unhelpful self-talk so we can redirect our thinking.

- The Journalist's Approach helps us question the validity of a negative or limiting statement so we can open up our perspective.

- We have to be our own best cheerleader.

PART 2

QUIET CAPITAL FRAMEWORK

So far, we've outlined the friction many of us feel when we take our Quiet Culture traits and apply them in a Loud Culture working world. We've shared strategies for how we can rethink our approach by leaning in to our Cultural Reframes. Now, in part 2, we focus on building strategic visibility at work, because while our Cultural Reframes may open our eyes, they might not necessarily open doors. To give our Cultural Reframes legs, we have to focus on what we can do when we are at work. Enter the Quiet Capital Framework. This is a three-pillar construct that positions us to be noticed the way we want to be. By shaping our career brand, establishing credibility, and advocating for ourselves, we are taking a proactive approach to gaining the recognition we deserve.

CHAPTER 4

SHAPING OUR CAREER BRAND

Controlling the narrative of our work

When you step into a TV newsroom, the chaos and noise are exactly how you would imagine them. TVs are blaring, phones are ringing, the radio is broadcasting, and people are bustling around left and right. Editors are alerting producers about the latest breaking news, and producers are instructing reporters on what to do so they don't miss a beat. The environment is the epitome of a Loud Culture. For a young college grad raised with Quiet Culture values, stepping into this new environment was quite overwhelming. Everything I knew about the world, from the textbooks I'd read in school to what my parents had told me to do, failed to prepare me for this reality.

As a result, when I started working, I had little idea of how to carry myself to get noticed, let alone be seen the way I wanted to be. It wasn't that I didn't *like* the loud, busy environment, it was that I simply didn't know how to exist in it. The speed at which people were working felt intimidating. The way they would discuss, debate, and even disagree with each other loudly in meetings (and even with my manager!) was jarring. I found myself constantly questioning whether it was OK to do something. Because I had no clear answer, I found myself caving in to stay within the bounds of what I knew. If you can imagine it, this is what my day looked like: I would go into the office, sit in meetings quietly, take instructions, and go about my day alone. I worked by myself—researching, interviewing, and writing. In the TV world, there's actually a name for this. They call it being a one-man band, and that was me to a T.

However, this idea of doing things alone completely flipped when I was given my first big TV breaking news assignment at NBC in Reno. On this Tuesday morning, a blaring alert came through the office: There had been a huge train crash about forty miles outside the city. Multiple people were presumed dead. National TV networks like CNN were calling our office for more information. With nothing else to go on, I packed my bags to head straight to the scene.

Just as I was about to step out the door, my boss shouted from across the newsroom, "Vanessa and Justin are going with you!"

Vanessa was a veteran journalist and Justin was a seasoned photographer, and both had years of experience in the industry. But when I heard they were coming, I couldn't help but wonder why.

"It's a big story and we need all hands on deck," my manager finished.

As we drove together, I kept thinking about how I didn't need help with the story. I was worried that because there were three of us, it was now going to take longer to coordinate and get the job done.

Once we arrived, we learned that a truck driver, distracted by his cell phone, had slammed into an Amtrak train at a railroad crossing. The scene was chaotic. Police cars, fire engines, ambulances, and news vans were parked on the side of the road. First responders were tending to the injured. Six people were presumed dead. In the distance, a large fire was still blazing from the wrecked train.

Without giving ourselves much time to process the immensity of the crash, the three of us got to work. Vanessa found passengers to interview, Justin focused on shooting B-roll, and I went to look for police officers and firefighters to gather information.

Within fifteen minutes, we reconvened and prepared to go live on TV. Justin set up the camera and Vanessa and I alternated between speaking, giving updates, and adding context to the story. Whatever I said, she complemented it with eyewitness accounts. The stories we each presented were made so much stronger because we worked on them together.

Once we wrapped up, the three of us got back into the car. It was going to be at least an hour-long drive back to the office, so I thought I would sneak in a nap. Just as I was about to doze off, Vanessa turned toward me and said, "Hey—really great job today."

"Thanks—you too!" I chimed back.

As I shut my eyes, I smiled. I appreciated that she acknowledged my work. It also felt great to return the compliment. Then it hit me—we were able to celebrate each other because we had been there *together*. She had seen firsthand how I handled myself in such a chaotic situation, and I had witnessed a pro in action. But more important, we now had a shared experience, which deepened our connection to each other. In that moment, I realized that maybe I needed to rethink the strategy of just working hard and working alone.

Later, as we got back to the office, I overheard Vanessa debriefing our manager.

"Oh, Jessica did great! She is a really fast worker," she said.

It was a simple compliment, but coming from a veteran reporter who was well respected in our office, it solidified my capabilities. It also carried more weight because it was said by someone my boss trusted. So the question now was: How could I take this experience and find more opportunities like it to accelerate my career growth?

This is where we kick off the first pillar of our Quiet Capital Framework. If our Cultural Reframes helped us rethink how we approach work, then our Quiet Capital Framework is what will help us build influence and visibility. Because when we arm ourselves with the right mindset and tools, we get noticed the way we want to be. It all starts with shaping our career brand.

YOUR CAREER BRAND

It was a Tuesday morning, and as I sat down at my desk and opened up Zoom, Charity Waterson and her team from Microsoft were already waiting on the other end. She had just attended a workshop I hosted at Microsoft where I taught employees how to build their career brand. She loved it and wanted to provide this exact training to her team of engineers.

"Many of our WebXT engineers are smart and hardworking, but they need help thinking about how to position themselves so they can talk about their work," said Waterson.

"I get it," I responded. "Working hard is not a career brand. Working hard is expected. A career brand is what others think of us when we're not in the room."

Over the next few weeks, we worked on crafting two sessions for her team: one for managers to learn how to position themselves and empower others to do the same, and the other for individual contributors to learn how to market themselves for visibility. Together, we called the sessions "Cracking Your Career Code."

One of the things we touched upon in the training was ensuring that everyone knew they could have full control over creating a career brand they were proud of. Because a career brand isn't just a title, a role, or even how hard we work. A career brand is something we can use as a North Star to guide *what* kind of work we do, with *whom* we do it, and *how* we can position ourselves for greater visibility in the office. Upon first glance, building a career brand may sound unachievable. "We can't control the kind of work we do" or "We just do as we're told" are some of the responses I get from skeptics. But it's quite the opposite. We have more ownership over how people perceive us as long as we take the appropriate steps. The key is to be intentional with *what* we do with the work we're given, so we can maximize every opportunity—big or small. If this sounds like how we reframed Spend Time, that's because it is— we're putting our reframes into action now.

To shape our career brand, we first have to rethink our Quiet Culture mentality of not talking about our capabilities. In fact, one of the most fascinating insights I came across while interviewing leaders for this book was that the reason many of them got to where they are was not because of their book smarts, their education, or their work speed. They got to their positions because they could take what they were given and shape it to new opportunities, new connections, and therefore, more influence for themselves. But to do it in a way that feels right, we have to get clear on the things we *value*. According to researchers, when we do work we enjoy, see the value in it, and feel connected to its purpose, we feel a kind of organizational bond called affective commitment. The by-product of this is feeling more fulfilled and satisfied, thus elevating our performance.

So, building your career brand starts with identifying your core values, which we will do together. This exercise will take some work up front, which most of us never give ourselves the time to do, but it will be well worth it. Once we identify your core values, we can then talk about identifying your differentiating factor, linking talent to opportunity, and expanding your reach. Together, these four steps shape your career brand, and it is something you can use to showcase yourself and be proud of at work.

CAREER BRAND

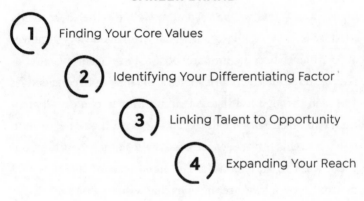

1. Finding Your Core Values
2. Identifying Your Differentiating Factor
3. Linking Talent to Opportunity
4. Expanding Your Reach

STEP 1: Finding Your Core Values

The first step to building your career brand is getting crystal clear about the things you value. This is where you have to get brutally honest. What values do you find most meaningful and fulfilling? What are you motivated by? Brené Brown, author and leadership expert, writes in her book *Dare to Lead,* "Our values should be so crystallized in our minds, so infallible, so precise and clear and unassailable, that they don't feel like a choice—they are simply a definition of who we are in our lives."

At first glance, you may wonder how career brand values differ from our Quiet Culture values. Quiet Culture values are those we were taught to embody because of how we were raised.

They're neither good nor bad, they're just a part of who we are today. Career brand values, on the other hand, are those that drive the kind of work we do because it fulfills an inner purpose. Our career brand values give us direction and energy so that no matter how busy we get, we don't feel drained, tired, or demoralized. Instead, we start the day knowing why we're doing the work, and we want to do it well. Furthermore, when what we care about aligns with what we are good at, our power and influence become unmatched. So, to get clear on your career brand values, here are some terms for you to consider. As you read through the list, it is important to choose no more than two or three that call to you the most. It will be difficult to keep to this limit, because many will sound important, but you'll want to stay focused. Get honest about the ones that matter to you. These are the ones that will become your career brand beacon and will be sacrosanct to everything you do.

Achievement	Growth	Quality
Analysis	Honesty	Recognition
Balance	Independence	Relaxation
Challenge	Influence	Research
Competition	Integrity	Respect
Creativity	Leadership	Risk-taking
Diversity	Learning	Spirituality
Efficiency	Management	Status
Financial Stability	Perseverance	Structure
Flexibility	Physicality	Support
Freedom	Power	Teamwork
Friendship	Predictability	Trust

For me, the two core values that feel the most true to who I am are freedom and growth. But having been raised with Quiet Culture values, embodying the core value of freedom was difficult to practice, even though it felt right deep down. Because I had a hard time saying no and creating boundaries for myself, I wondered if freedom could really be one of my core values. For example, when others would ask for help, I would always say yes, because I didn't want to rock the boat and cause conflict. Unsurprisingly, I often found myself drained and burned out; although I was helping others, I wasn't giving myself the freedom of choice, which I truly longed for. However, once I realized and accepted that one of my core values was indeed freedom, I became immensely more intentional with my time and how I used it. I started asking questions like: If I have to do this work, how can I use it to position myself for the projects I actually want to do? How can I rearrange my time so I can give myself some semblance of control to do work that makes me happy? How can I find the courage to gracefully say no to certain busywork so I can do work that excites me? This last one was scary, because I didn't know the ramifications of saying no, but I trusted that as long as I was smart about it, it meant a happier and better-working me. (It is important to note that saying no can be tricky, because if not handled properly, it can actually hurt our career brand. That's why I cover the art of confidently saying no in chapter 6.)

Growth was an easy core value for me to identify and easier to apply to my daily work. I've always been curious about people—why we do the things we do and how things come to be. I've always enjoyed the quiet nature of learning and listening. Thinking about immersing myself in a new book to expand my thinking or taking on a new hobby (hello, harp!) is something I still relish, because growth means new experiences. When it came time to choose an industry, journalism was the perfect place to start my career, because every day was a new adventure. One day I would be learning about politics, the next day I would be immersed in business news, and the following day I would be diving headfirst into a health care story. Work that will spur my growth will always be a motivating factor for me. So, what are your core values? Write them down here:

Core Value 1: _____

Core Value 2: _____

Core Value 3: _____

STEP 2: Identifying Your Differentiating Factor

The second step to shaping your career brand is to identify your differentiating factor. To do this, reflect on the kind of work you *enjoy* doing, particularly what you're good at. Think back over the past three months and consider what got you excited and what came naturally to you. Chances are you might not have enjoyed every aspect of your work, but there were certain tasks and projects you probably gladly jumped into and did with ease. It could've been your technical skills with numbers and data, your expertise in a certain area, or your writing skills. Hint: What you enjoy doing is probably what you're good at. It's what people call finding their flow. The work comes easily and the time passes quickly. If you're not sure, answer the following questions to dig a little deeper to find your differentiating factor.

When you start work every morning, what do you find yourself wanting to do first? (*E.g., My favorite part of the day is looking at a blank sheet of paper and sketching some fresh design ideas I have in my mind.*)

_____

_____

When the manager assigns the team a project, what role do you find yourself gravitating toward? (*E.g., I like writing the final report, because I like to take what everyone did and connect the dots.*)

_____

_____

What's something that comes easily to you at work—that is, you instinctively "get it"? (*E.g., I'm on the data analysis team, so seeing* *large amounts of data isn't intimidating. Rather, I see it as a puzzle to put together.)*

_____

_____

As you reflect on your answers, you may discover a theme. You may even have more than one differentiating factor. That is great. Your differentiating factor is your competitive advantage, because not only do you like the work, you're also good at it. Don't assume that what comes naturally to you is easy for others. There is no right or wrong answer here. What's important is that whatever your differentiating factor is, you are happy to be known for it, because your career brand will be anchored in it. What you want people to say is, "We need someone to help with XYZ; [your name] is the person for it!"

In my case, my differentiating factor as a journalist was my ability to cover business stories. I would get most excited when I was assigned a story related to commerce, industry, and markets. I also had a knack for it. I could take dry business issues and bring them to life. I also developed the skill to dig through dense financial reports, find patterns, and humanize the data to make it relatable. Before I knew it, I had a large contact list of businesses and executives I could call on whenever our TV station needed to do an economy-driven story. The way I exercised my differentiating factor was twofold. First, I always presented at least one business story idea in meetings so I could create that career brand recognition. Second, if my colleagues needed help with a business story, I would jump in and spend time helping them. Before I knew it, whenever a business story came into the office, I was the first person who came to mind. Business news effectively became my career brand, and I was happy about it.

STEP 3: Linking Talent to Opportunity

At this point, you've identified your core values and your differentiating factor. Together, these make up *talent*. When what you're good at aligns with what you find value in, you have unstoppable energy. The work feels right and you feel happy doing it. But here's the thing: while you may be known as the data person, the brilliant engineer, or the writer who can string together words artfully, these are just skills. You may love doing these things, and they may come naturally to you, but the reality is, (most) skills can be duplicated by someone else. It is why when layoffs and consolidations happen at work, your ability to execute alone will not protect you from being eliminated. Instead, the ones who give themselves a fighting chance are those who can marry their talent with intangible skills. Intangible skills are things like communication, problem-solving, emotional intelligence, and the ability to collaborate.

As a matter of fact, when you start applying your Cultural Reframes at work, you will find that you're exercising your intangible skills too. For example, when you communicate by tailoring your message to your audience and what they care about (Engage Others), you are showcasing your *communication skills*. When you take the work you're doing and maximize every opportunity (Spend Time), you are demonstrating your ability to *influence*. When you share how your work benefits the greater good (Handle Wins), you are proving you can make an *impact*. And when you handle confrontation by focusing on the dynamics at play (Manage Conflict), you are displaying incredible *emotional intelligence*.

One of the most influential ways to link talent to opportunity is to create the opportunities yourself. Like we talked about earlier, while we don't always get to choose the kind of work we do, we do have the ability to pitch and create even small projects that can demonstrate our ability to think big. Because it's during these times, when we weren't asked to do something but we did it anyway, that we can make the most lasting impression. It doesn't have to be a grand plan or even a huge project, but just showing our proactiveness of thinking beyond the day-to-day can give us an edge. For me, I realized that if I wanted to demonstrate my intangible skills, I needed to carve out that opportunity for myself; the truth was, while I wanted my career brand to be as a business expert, *anyone* could be seen as a business expert. My ability to bring dry business stories to life, while a differentiating factor, was not unique to me. I did it well because I cared about doing it well, but anyone could come in and do the same. So I went back to my two core values of freedom and growth, and I started asking questions to help me create an invaluable opportunity for myself and the team. For example, if freedom was important to me, how could I give myself the space and time to focus on work I *wanted* to do? Next, growth. What kinds of projects could I challenge myself with creating that demonstrated I was more than just a typical business reporter?

What I came up with while working at a television station in the greater New York City area was conceptualizing, pitching, and creating an entirely new business show from scratch. There was nothing like it at the time, so I took the initiative to create my own opportunity. By putting my name to a business project, I knew I could solidify how people thought of me. I didn't want to be known just as a business expert, who could easily be replaced by another; I wanted to *show* that I could innovate, problem-solve, and create business value too. Similarly, if you want to be seen as an irreplaceable expert, you've got to start living and showcasing your career brand. Whether it's through your Cultural Reframes or creating your own opportunities, know that the ball is in your court to make your career brand stick.

STEP 4: Expanding Your Reach

The final step to shaping your career brand is to expand your reach. While *you* may know where your talent lies and you are finding ways to demonstrate it through innovative work, teamwork, and collaboration, will others remember it? The key to shaping and living your career brand is to know it is a never-ending process. Consistency is the key ingredient to cementing a memorable career brand that people will remember. I actually like to think of it as a flywheel. With every step of your career brand established, you can now continually find ways to bring it up, including talking about what you're good at, so others can see and keep you top of mind. Because in my experience, our influence compounds to even bigger opportunities as long as we are visible.

How this looks in the real world is best told with the story of Michael Chen, the former president and CEO of General Electric's Media, Communications, and Entertainment division. We met him in the very beginning of this book when he shared the story of Kevin, who was expecting a promotion but was passed over. How Chen shaped his own career brand and leveraged it to eventually become CEO, managing a $7 billion business, was no accident.

A few years into his job at General Electric, where Chen was sitting as a mid-level risk manager, he began itching for more. He started to dream about what it would take to be CEO one day. It was a bold dream, but it was one he wanted to make a reality. So he started mapping out a career brand that would help get him there. Chen identified his core values, which were building relationships and being a value-add to others. He then identified what came naturally to him, his differentiating factor—his ability to take mass amounts of data and make them meaningful—and he used his talent to expand his reach to other people in other departments. His first target: the sales team.

"I would reach out and say, 'I don't have anything, but I just want to spend a few minutes understanding how I can help you,'" said Chen.

He said he wanted to learn the ins and outs of sales so he could bolster his business expertise. In exchange, he took his differentiating factor and offered to analyze data for the sales team for free.

"I went to the head of sales and said, 'I'm creating this credit information for customers with my boss, but I can also put in sales information so they can access their information as well,'" Chen explained. "I spent about a year working on this project, and I was working probably eighty hours a week because during the day I was trying to build these new relationships with sales, but I still had to get my [risk] work done."

While he was building new relationships, Chen was simultaneously demonstrating his intangible skills of cross-collaboration and communication. "I met every single client in North America, and I dealt with every single salesperson. They liked me because I was helping them create this database," he said.

Eventually, he found himself in the right place at the right time. The head of sales for North America was retiring, and Chen's name was thrown into the mix. Because he was visible and had shown he was capable, he was chosen for the new sales role, despite never having climbed the traditional sales ladder. But the story didn't end there. As Chen's career progressed, so did his career brand and influence. As the new head of sales for North America, he now had access to some of the company's top clients: airline companies and their executives. This meant a new group of people who knew him and whom he could engage with.

"The turning point came when one of the [airline] CEOs actually called the CEO of GE . . . and said they should promote me," Chen said. "At that time I was six levels below the CEO of GE, so he had no idea who I was. But when a peer of his, a CEO of a major airline, called him up and told him about me, all of a sudden my CEO wanted to know who I was. I didn't promote myself; my clients promoted me."

While there was certainly a level of luck and good timing involved, because Chen positioned himself well and was ready for an opportunity to arise, he got it. At every step of the way, he leveraged his differentiating factor and demonstrated his intangible skills. He did this all while staying true to his core value of being a value-add, while finding opportunities to continually expand his reach.

"My strategy was to build relationships," he said. "I really liked interacting with people and I really cared about building their business in a genuine way. I built a genuine relationship with the CEOs of the airlines. We had dinner together, went to events together, and became personal friends."

For Chen, his ascension did not come by going at it alone. He ascended because he found that the more he gave, the more he got. He certainly did not leave his career brand to chance— if he had, he might have stayed firmly planted in his risk-department role. But more important, he was proactive about it. Like a flywheel, his influence kept going and going.

By giving yourself the time to reflect on the four steps of shaping your career brand, you are taking an intentional approach to how you show up in the workplace. When you do work that aligns with your values, while emphasizing your intangible skills, you are creating the kind of impact you want, which can make working in a Loud Culture world much more seamless. Because here's the thing: if you don't do this, other people will do it for you. They will begin to brand you in a way that suits them, whether intentionally or not. For instance, you will be known as the go-to person for X kind of project, because people know you can do it—but it's not the kind of work you actually want to do. So remember, you are the captain of your own ship, and you are in control of where you want it to go. With the first step of the Quiet Capital Framework in place, we now move on to the second: building credibility at work.

The Power of Making Connections

Gloria Lee, client relations partner at Rutan & Tucker (the largest full-service law firm in Orange County, California), is a great example of someone who identified their differentiating factor and used it to develop their career brand. When you meet Gloria, the phrase that often comes to mind is, "You know everyone!" She is a master connector.

But it wasn't always this way. When Gloria first graduated from law school and started working, she discovered that she was one of thousands who had a great degree and a good job. Yes, she could write Stanford University and the University of California, Berkeley, on her résumé, but she knew it wasn't enough to help her stand out in a crowded workplace. Or if anything were to happen to the firm or if the economy went into a recession, she could easily be cut.

"There are basic requirements of the job you have to show—you're hardworking, you're smart, you're responsive, you're a good writer," said Gloria. "But that doesn't mean they're not going to lay you off. They can find anyone to do the job."

Gloria knew she had to set herself apart. While she had grown up with Quiet Culture values and was very much expected to embody them at home, when at work, she leveraged her Cultural Reframes and doubled down on how she engaged others and spent time. She cared about building connections with people, and she loved connecting people with each other. So, through time, she strategically amassed a large network of friends and started making introductions that would help other people. Gloria said the time spent providing value and listening to what other people needed resulted in friends turning into clients.

As her network expanded, Gloria also started getting more opportunities to speak at conferences. As a junior attorney, she was able to showcase her differentiating factor, which was her ability to speak well, talk about the law, and link it to wider industry trends. She could also connect the dots between what her clients wanted and the resources she had.

"I showed them I had these intangible qualities, which are much harder to find," Gloria said. "As a junior attorney, you're not necessarily bringing in a lot of clients, but how do you demonstrate those qualities? I say, 'Hey, my friend is the CEO of this company and is asking about these legal issues, can I introduce you?' Or 'I've been asked to speak at an event, would you like to present with me?'"

Gloria realized that the more she spoke, the more people she met, the more visible she became, and thus the more her career brand was taking shape, like a flywheel in motion.

"I'm not the successful entrepreneur type . . . but all my friends are," Gloria said. "So I connect them. I help them in a unique and creative way, so when people say, 'Hey, you're friends with Gloria,' they'll say, 'She will hook you up.' It's how I give to others.

"It's reminding them you are not only a great warrior, but you have this community and network that may be different from theirs."

WORD TO THE WISE

 The steps needed to shape your career brand don't have to feel overwhelming. The first thing you can do is simply ask yourself what you want to be known for. Here's a quick Q&A to help you get started:

- When someone hears your name, what *words* do you want them to think of? (Choose three.)
- What can you *do at work* to exhibit these qualities? (List three action items.)

That's it! Leading with what you want to be known for can be a guiding light to showing up the way you want to be seen. Now go out and start shaping your career brand.

THE BOTTOM LINE

- Shaping our career brand is the first pillar of our Quiet Capital Framework.

- Our career brand is our reputation and the positive things people will say about us when we're not in the room.

- If we don't shape our career brand, other people will shape it for us.

- Career brand step 1: Find your core values.

- Career brand step 2: Identify your differentiating factor.

- Career brand step 3: Link talent to opportunity.

- Career brand step 4: Expand your reach.

CHAPTER 5

BUILDING CREDIBILITY

Gaining respect and trust at work

"Mom, help!" I yelled from across the room.

The year was 1995, and it was the day after Christmas. My younger brother, Eric, and I were knee-deep in building a Lego set we had just gotten for the holidays, but thirty minutes in, we hit trouble.

"I know what to do!" my brother said as my mom walked in. "I told you already, the pieces go here. I've done this before, and I know how it works!"

Instinctively, I shrugged off my brother's suggestion and looked at my mom. As the older sister, I thought if I couldn't figure it out, surely my younger brother couldn't either.

"What's going on here?" my mom said.

"I think this piece goes here, but Eric said it goes the other way," I replied. "Can you help us?"

My mom picked up the Legos and quickly put them down.

"I am not really sure, but Eric, listen to whatever your jie jie says."

"Jie jie" in Chinese means "older sister," and in the confines of an Asian home, it was not surprising my mom defaulted to having me lead the way. At home, it was understood that my brother should follow whatever I said because I was older. It was the traditional thing to do, and it was also the respectful thing to show. For many of us raised with Quiet Culture traits, we see deference to authority similarly because following whomever is more senior is expected at home and in the workplace. It is why, early on when I started working, I was shocked to see some of my Loud Culture colleagues discussing, challenging, and even debating with those who were more senior in the office. They would challenge the way things were done, dismiss assignments given to them, and even state how they had better ideas to pursue. Privately, I thought: How could they be so bold? How could they question authority so unabashedly? How were they not afraid of getting reprimanded for speaking up to senior leaders? The Quiet Culture in me couldn't quite comprehend it, but perhaps more shockingly, I saw that my colleagues who did it weren't discouraged from it; rather, they were *respected* for having a strong point of view. It was shocking to see this dynamic because it was completely different from what I had been taught to do.

But back at home on that post-Christmas morning, the situation at hand had a real-life consequence to a five- and seven-year-old. My mom's attempt to solve the dilemma between me and my brother resulted in her doing what came naturally to her. However, the truth was, my brother, despite being younger, was more experienced with Legos than me. And from the corner of my eye, I do remember him sitting there waiting, his eyes likely rolling in frustration as I haphazardly tried to lead the way.

I share this lighthearted story because, while silly, the real-life takeaway is that many of us raised with Quiet Culture traits use hierarchy as a way to measure how we act around others. At work, we see age, the number of years worked, or someone's title, and we think that because it's *more* or *higher* than ours, we have to acquiesce and follow them. In fact, there is a term to describe this focus on hierarchy: *power distance*, which is the inclination to think about rank, authority, and where we fit into the social construct to understand ourselves and how we should behave. In *high* power-distance cultures, a junior person will unfailingly defer to the higher-ranking person, accepting what they say as truth. But in *low* power-distance cultures, everyone is treated with the same level of consideration, regardless of background or title. For example, in a Loud Culture workplace, it is not surprising to see a junior analyst hold considerable sway over the decision-making process because they have a unique experience or perspective, and everyone recognizes that.

This is where we enter our second pillar of the Quiet Capital Framework: building credibility. For those of us raised with Quiet Culture traits, talking about building credibility is important because we have to rethink how this is done in order for us to get noticed for all the right reasons. Right now, we may instinctively fall victim to authority bias and think whoever is in command is always right. Similarly, we may shrink our own contributions and expertise and give way to others because we assume, just based on their title, that they know more. Or we may feel intimidated, shy, and timid around senior leaders when really, there is no need to be, especially if we know our stuff. Learning how to build credibility can arm us with the right tools so we don't default to feeling lesser than just because we are more junior. Personally, it took me years to figure out how to strategically build my own credibility and confidence. But I knew I had to do this because just agreeing all the time, quietly following the rules, and deferring to others was not building my credibility in a Loud Culture workplace.

So the question is: What is credibility and what does it take to establish it at work? According to leadership experts James M. Kouzes and Barry Z. Posner, credibility is our reputation, and it is something that is earned over time. We also need to have trust and respect, because without it, people won't listen to us, believe in us, or follow us.

Credibility = Respect + Trust

To break down this formula even further, let's look specifically at how respect and trust are built, and what characteristics are needed to demonstrate them at work. In the following section, we will do a deep dive into how we can gain respect, and how we can build trust in front of our team, including how to handle ourselves in tricky situations. At a high level, it's asking ourselves these two questions: What are we *doing*? And What are we *saying*?

RESPECT: THE ACTION WE TAKE

The word *respect* can mean many things. It's respect for people and their ideas, their individuality, their boundaries, and their beliefs. However, what's less talked about is that respect can also be cultivated through the actions we take. Respect is not just something that passively happens; it is something that is actively obtained through the things we *do* and *show*.

Remember Cheryl Cheng, whom we met in chapter 2, when she navigated the high-stakes situation of killing an important project in front of her team? With her credibility on the line, she had to tread carefully, because she didn't want to catch her team off guard, potentially damaging their perception of her. So, through time, she primed them with careful questions, and eventually got them to realize that hitting their goal was not going to happen. Cheng's story is a great example of the Cultural Reframes of Manage Conflict and Engage Others at work. However, during my conversation with her, she also shared a story of when she learned that actions, without the proper cultural context, can have unintended consequences.

Growing up in a Quiet Culture, Cheng said that whenever family or guests were around, her natural instinct was to be hospitable and helpful, especially with elders. She demonstrated this by taking on simple tasks like offering food or water as a way of showing respect. While this was an attentive and even an expected gesture in the context of a Quiet Culture, when applied in a Loud Culture workplace, it gave a very different impression.

Cheng said one day, when she was working at an investment banking firm right after college, she was pulled into a meeting with her manager and clients. As she sat down, she noticed water was missing from the table. Instinctively, she jumped up and asked if anyone in the room wanted something to drink.

"It was a reflex, like, a natural thing," recalled Cheng.

She quickly ran out, grabbed the water, and set it on the table for everyone. But what had seemed like a benign thing to do, she said, had unintended consequences. After that meeting, her managing director pulled her aside.

"He said, 'I never want to see you ask that question again,'" Cheng recalled. "He said when I did that, I was reinforcing that I was more junior."

Stunned at the misalignment of her action and how it was perceived, Cheng said she understood what he was saying. Her managing director was telling her that during this critical time when she was in front of stakeholders, she needed to maximize her face-to-face time by making a strong impression.

"He said, 'If you ever want people to *respect* you, you have to think about every single cue you give them.'"

When thinking about cues and gaining respect at work, what can we do to demonstrate we've got what it takes? At baseline, we have to be able to execute the work assigned to us and do it well. There is no point trying to gain the respect of our colleagues if our deliverables are shoddy or littered with mistakes.

But just as important, how can we be thoughtful with the actions we take so people respect us and our capabilities? The answer is in how we carry ourselves around others, specifically, demonstrating both *character-driven* attributes and *expertise-driven* attributes. Character-driven attributes are things like reliability, punctuality, and empathy. We show up, we listen, and we demonstrate we're present. Expertise-driven attributes are things like competence, communications, and problem-solving skills. Just like how we reframed Handle Wins, we've got to get good at showing what we know so people recognize it. We can't assume people will just *know*. In fact, awareness and visibility are integral parts of gaining respect and credibility at work. As Cheng's manager said, we have to think about every single cue we give people, especially in a high-stakes situation. Here are some examples of demonstrating expertise-driven attributes:

- Being present in the room by making small talk with those around us
- Talking about industry-related news to show our understanding of the market
- Giving presentations at work
- Deciding where to sit during in-person meetings, including in more visible seats, not hidden in the back or to the side

- Having our camera turned on and our positioning, lighting, and background clean and professional in virtual meetings

These attributes are not loud or forced, but they are intentional, so when others see us, we act and look like the experts we are in our field. For Cheng, hindsight was twenty-twenty. In retrospect, what she should've done was engage in small talk with her clients, talk about the latest market trends, or take any action that would've demonstrated she was a critical member of the team, which she was. As for the missing water, the better measure would have been to ask the receptionist to grab it for the team. When others are around, our presence and what we show is the basis for how respect is built.

TRUST: THE WORDS WE SAY

Every single driver in America is required to have car insurance when operating a car. The car insurance industry as a whole is worth $316 billion, according to IBISWorld. For most of us, it's an annual payment that's painful to shell out, but when we need it, we are so thankful we have it. Talking about our work is just like having car insurance. We may feel like it is superfluous because it takes time and effort, but doing so can protect us when things go bad.

Obviously, it's easier to talk about our work when things are going well. We're in a good mood and we're feeling confident, and simple, "just letting you know" check-ins are all we need. But when things go south, what do we do? How do we communicate the status without sabotaging the impression people have of us? The answer is, we have to double down on communicating the process, even if it feels incredibly hard to do so. Because without it, *trust* won't exist.

As with respect, there are some baseline criteria we have to meet before others will trust us and our expertise. At minimum, trust is built on good faith. It also can take time. But if we're talking about communicating, looping others in to what we're doing is key. Admittedly, as a young reporter, I learned this the hard way. I did not have the foresight to communicate when things got tricky. Instead, I tried to troubleshoot things alone because I was scared of looking incompetent. But as a result, building trust with my team fell to the wayside multiple times. In one particular instance, I told my manager I was going to be ready to deliver a news story by a certain time. But from that morning, I knew I had overfilled my plate. (Yes, I defaulted to thinking I needed to tack on a lot of work to prove I was hardworking.) On this day, I had clearly miscalculated, and I was hitting roadblocks and had to pivot many times. Instead of talking about it, I leaned in to my Quiet Culture nature and kept the problem to myself, trying to fix it alone. But managing the situation myself completely affected my timing. I missed the deadline. In TV, a missed deadline can cause a big ripple effect. Back in the office, I knew that as a result of my miss, I had left my manager with the impossible task of scrambling to adjust everyone's schedule with only minutes to spare.

In hindsight, what I should've done was talk about the road-blocks as they were happening. Doing so could've helped me and my manager problem-solve together. But because I didn't, it was a mess, and the trust he had in me and my abilities cracked.

Our reluctance to engage in conflict, and our desire to save face or not be a bother, can be strong forces, especially for those of us raised with Quiet Culture traits. However, the difference between us and our Loud Culture colleagues is that they acknowledge and accept that tricky conversations are bound to happen. They know it's just part of the job. They do it not because they think it's easy, but because they don't want to catch people when it's too late. They want to proactively tackle the problem, like they are playing offense, not defense. But for those of us raised with Quiet Culture values, the desire to maintain a harmonious environment, not lose face, or not disappoint others can keep us from speaking up, and we avoid addressing the situation at all. But the quickest way to shatter the trust people have in us is to involve them when it's too late, or fail to loop them in at all.

Mei Xu, founder of Chesapeake Bay Candle, one of the most popular candle brands in the US, shared a poignant story with me that highlights how haphazardly she learned how to talk about her work, especially during tough times. Xu was a guest on our Soulcast Media | LIVE show, and she shared how this lesson revealed itself in an embarrassing moment with one of her biggest buyers, Target. Chesapeake Bay Candle was a small business at the time, so Xu was thrilled a big-box retailer wanted to carry her product. This was an opportunity she knew could change the trajectory of her company. So when Target asked if she could fulfill a $1 million candle order, Xu quickly reached out to her sister, who was operating their factory in China, to see if it was doable. Together, they agreed they had to seize the opportunity and make it work.

"Sure, no problem," Xu told the reps at Target.

The sisters, who were raised with Quiet Culture traits, made it a priority to please their new client, whom they saw as their "superior" because Target had the buying power. They wanted to convey the image that everything was fine and not lose the trust the company had in them. But in reality, behind the scenes, it was chaos. Their factory was not equipped to handle such a big order due to the variety of textiles, glass, and wax colors needed.

Xu said that instead of communicating their manufacturing and supply troubles, she leaned in to her Quiet Culture tendency to avoid conflict and didn't say a thing. She and her team tried to troubleshoot the problems themselves, but their deadline was getting harder and harder to meet. Xu reflected that her communication style, or lack thereof, caused a lot of mistrust, including being seen as shady.

"To someone coming from a straight-shooting Midwestern-American context, such misrepresentation was dishonest," Xu said, reflecting on her buyer's perspective.

"After only one complete retail season, Target's buyers, merchandisers, and managers taught this confrontation-averse Asian not just to communicate, but to overcommunicate," said Xu.

After this experience, Xu said, what helped her was reframing her communication approach so it was less about the power distance between her and her buyer. Instead, it was about see-ing both sides as partners helping each other succeed. This new perspective allowed her to feel more comfortable being commu-nicative and transparent, thus creating more trust between her and Target as they continued their partnership together.

Talking about our work and what's happening is not only smart, it's strategic. Letting others know what's happening and being honest, especially when things are not working out, is one of the best things to build and maintain trust. When we communicate roadblocks, we give others a chance to step in and help. When we approach the situation with a "let's figure this out together" mindset versus an "it's too late" reaction, the impression sticks. I've learned unequivocally that manag-ers prefer the former.

So in terms of building trust to maintain our credibility, I now want to get tactical about *how* we can communicate, spe-cifically in tricky situations, so you know what to do and what to say. We can accomplish this by using the TACT Framework.

TACT FRAMEWORK

In a Loud Culture workplace, building credibility takes work. We know it is earned and it requires the respect and trust of others. We also know being thoughtful and strategic is what anchors both. Similarly, to become tactful communicators when things don't go as planned, we have to know *how* to deliver the news with sensitivity and discretion, so our credibility doesn't crack. To do this, it helps to understand the difference between *effective* versus *appropriate* communication. Effective communication is providing information that is needed so others know what's going on; appropriate communication is considering the context surrounding the situation. An example of appropriate communication is gauging who is involved and what the purpose of a meeting is *before* we speak, while effective communication is providing the data and evidence to back up our points *when* we speak. For many of us, we may never break down our communication in this way, especially when dealing with tough situations, but it is a holistic approach for better speaking.

So how do we apply this at work and what does it sound like? Enter the TACT Framework, which is a sequence of considerations that can help us leverage both appropriate and effective communication so we have a strategic game plan. TACT stands for: **T**ake a moment, **A**rticulate the process, **C**ommunicate solutions, and **T**alk it out together.

COMMUNICATING DIFFICULT SITUATIONS

T   Take a moment

A   Articulate the process

C   Communicate solutions

T   Talk it out together

T: Take a moment

When we realize things are not going as planned and we start feeling anxious, our body will tense up and our mind will start running through a million different scenarios. Those of us who resonate with a Quiet Culture usually feel this tension because we are sensitive to conflict. When we take a moment, we acknowledge that while we may want to avoid the conflict, hiding is the quickest way to shatter our credibility. Instead, we need to take a moment to turn our thinking around, and lean in to our Cultural Reframe of Manage Conflict to evaluate the dynamics at play. Because it's not about avoiding conflict, it's about taking the time to get a temperature check in order to clearly see what's going on.

A: Articulate the process

Next, we have to articulate what exactly is going on to whomever we're speaking with. What we don't want to do is suddenly burst out with the negative news up front, because that may trigger unintended shockwaves. Others may think we're overreacting or that we're jumping the gun. Instead, we need to ask ourselves:

- What do people already know?
- What have we already done?
- What's the problem we're facing?

The answers to these questions can allow others to better understand what happened. This is the aforementioned appropriate communication at play, because we're carefully evaluating what's going on, what happened, and how best to share it. This is critical to maintaining our credibility, because the more others know, the better they can understand how things came to be.

Here's what articulating the process can look like using the two preceding stories as examples:

- Mei Xu's Target story: *We're beginning production of X amount of candles, but we wanted to let you know we've hit some unexpected manufacturing issues that might push our deadline back. I know it's not what you were hoping for, but we are taking ABC steps right now. We want to be fully transparent with you, so you know what's going on.*

  Note: Honest. Sharing steps taken. Not overpromising.

- My reporter deadline story: *I've been working on this story for a few hours now and I am not getting anywhere. I've reached out to A, B, and C already and have not heard back. I just wanted to give you a heads-up so you know we may need to pivot.*

  Note: Stated what has already been done. Stated what could be the outcome. Matter-of-fact.

C: Communicate solutions

After articulating the process, it's time to communicate solutions. An important step to maintaining our credibility is to not just communicate problems, but to offer ways forward, which is the effective communication we discussed earlier. While our manager may have the final say, it's helpful to present options for solutions up front. It shows we are thinking and keeping others in mind, because we are earnestly trying to problem-solve. Here's what this could sound like using the preceding examples:

- Mei Xu's Target story: *In the meantime, what I will do is connect with my team to discuss a plan B and I'll circle back with you next week.*

- My reporter deadline story: *I've already done some research and think this other story (A) might be another direction we can go. Or we can consider this one (B), because I remember there was interest in going that route too.*

Communicating solutions is a critical part of maintaining our credibility at work, because we are showing others that despite facing trouble, we are not hiding. Instead, we're thinking ahead. You might wonder, though, what if there is no solution to the problem yet? What if you're still trying to figure it out? The answer is to communicate your *process of thinking* in real time. For example, offering different paths for consideration, but prefacing it by saying it's still a work in progress. You can also include phrases like, "I'm thinking out loud here," or "I'm just brainstorming." This demonstrates that you're committed to fixing the problem, but you are still formulating your ideas. It is how you can show you're trying to be a problem-solver, not a problem-dumper.

T: Talk it out together

Ending your conversation with the space to answer questions is the fourth step in the TACT Framework. Talking it out together is accomplished by asking open-ended questions. This is important, because it does three things: it creates a space where discussion can happen, it allows for mutual understanding, and it loops others in to the decision-making process. The result is transparency and open communication. Here are some examples:

- Do you think that might work?
- Anything else you'd like to add?
- What are your thoughts?

There will also be times when we'll have to engage in difficult conversations when we least expect it. For example, our boss pulls us into a room or calls us unexpectedly to ask us a direct question we weren't prepared to answer. Or maybe our colleague puts us on the spot during a team meeting, demanding information we just don't have. In moments like these, we can feel like a deer in headlights. For those of us from a Quiet Culture, our heart may start pumping and we may nod our head in agreement just to get out of the glare. However, in these kinds of situations, practicing the TACT Framework is just as important. Even though all eyes are on us, taking a moment so we don't run or hide, articulating the process so we show we're engaged, communicating solutions so we display our problem-solving skills, and talking it out together can ensure our credibility stays intact. It's not about communicating in a loud way, it's about being TACT-ful. Building our credibility is not just what we do, it's also what we say and how we say it.

CREATING OUR ELEVATOR PITCH

In this chapter, we talked about respect and trust as integral ingredients for building and maintaining our credibility. We also talked about how we can communicate problems when they occur. However, building credibility also has a starting point—it begins the moment we meet someone new. Whether it's in a meeting, on a call, or at an event, when we meet someone for the first time, we have the opportunity to present ourselves in a way that can form the basis of how they feel about us. No one will actually say it, but when they meet us for the first time, they are likely analyzing what we have to say. One of the few times when it won't matter as much is if we are given a warm introduction by a credible source. But if we don't have that, people will be evaluating us and determining whether they want to spend the next few minutes talking to us, especially if they don't know us. Truth is, we are likely running through the exact same thoughts when we meet them. It's not malicious, it's just human nature.

This is why crafting our elevator pitch and knowing it ahead of time can give us a competitive advantage, especially in a new environment. Our elevator pitch doesn't have to be long or rehearsed, but having a framework can help us create a credible first impression. In fact, it's worth noting that in job interviews, we should be practicing our elevator pitch just as much as answering specific interview questions.

To create a dynamic elevator pitch, we first have to lean in to our Cultural Reframe of Handle Wins. We don't have to talk about ourselves in a loud or showy way; it is about embracing and sharing the amazing work we're doing and how it benefits others. More specifically, we have to package our accomplishments in a way that makes people want to pay attention. At its core, a great elevator pitch is clear and precise, and it's interesting enough that others want to know more.

Nanxi Liu is the co-founder and co-CEO at Blaze, a company that helps people build apps and tools without code. Before the age of twenty-five, she was named a Forbes 30 Under 30 and had already built two successful companies. Within ten years of graduating from college, Liu's second company, Enplug, was acquired by Spectrio, one of the nation's leading customer engagement technology providers. To say she has mastered establishing her elevator pitch as a tech and business expert at a young age is an understatement. While many young professionals might have shied away from talking about their work because they thought they were too young or too inexperienced, Liu did not let her age, or even the power distance, hold her back.

"I was able to get investors even as a senior in college," she shared one day as we jumped on a Zoom call. "There are always tidbits of credibility."

Liu said that as a student, while she didn't have the traditional workplace experience many associate with credibility, such as decades on the job or a prestigious corporate title, she didn't downplay the traits she did have. In her elevator pitch at networking events, she proudly shared that she was a student at UC Berkeley, had been elected to a school leadership position, and was building an app on the side, which two thousand people had already downloaded. While all these things may have sounded like small achievements to big investors, the point was she created the impression that she was a go-getter. Liu demonstrated she had the tenacity, talent, and energy to go above and beyond, and as we'll recall from the previous chapter on shaping our career brand, it's these intangible skills that can make us indispensable. And that's the thing: if we cannot get behind what we're working on and how it benefits others, how can we expect other people to?

Building your elevator pitch doesn't require you to be loud or boastful. You can still be humble and talk about your work with pride, as long as you talk about the benefits with conviction so others can see its value quickly.

To form the structure of your elevator pitch, we will break it down into four parts: teaser, headline, body, and takeaway. In fact, this structure is inspired by how those on TV communicate their news stories to capture the attention of viewers. Here's what the four elements look like in more detail:

1. **Teaser:** A few words that evoke emotion to attract the attention of others and set the tone. This should be tailored to your audience and what they care about.
2. **Headline:** High-level accomplishment to showcase what you've done that's unique to you and will impress others.
3. **Body:** Examples to prove your accomplishments, including numbers or timely stories to form context.
4. **Takeaway:** How you can help the person you're pitching, or a question to keep the dialogue going.

Here's an example of what an elevator pitch during an interview can sound like to show our capabilities:

INTERVIEWER: *Larry, can you tell me a little about yourself?*

ELEVATOR PITCH: So glad to be here, and I'd be happy to share [*teaser*]. I've been a software engineer for Google for almost five years now [*headline*]. I've specifically been with the payments platform team, where I helped manage the Ads, YouTube, and AdSense accounts, which are platforms that process billions of dollars every year [*body*]. The work has been great, but I am starting to explore the startup world because I know I can bring a lot to the table, which I am happy to talk about [*takeaway*].

Here's another example of an elevator pitch, during a panel setting:

MODERATOR: *Jenny, can you please share a little about yourself and the work you do with our audience?*

ELEVATOR PITCH: I'm delighted to be here today and to spend the afternoon with you all [*teaser*]. I've been researching the social implications of machine learning and AI for well over a decade now. Along with Margaret, we launched the world's first institute based in California dedicated to the environmental implications of AI [*headline*]. Since its creation, we've explored these core issues: how AI can be used to fight climate change, what industry AI is most concentrated in, and what its downsides are [*body*]. I'm excited to share more about what I've learned with everyone here today [*takeaway*].

Reading both examples, you'll notice the key to building a great elevator pitch is to stack the teaser, headline, body, and takeaway together, so they formulate an articulate message. Both pitches give just enough information for others to get a sense of who the person is, their accomplishments, and why they're credible. They also create intrigue, so others want to know more.

To help you build your elevator pitch, answer the following questions.

Teaser: What do you want the other person to feel after talking to you? Use words such as: *excited, happy, looking forward.* You can also leverage other emotions by using words like *concerned, shocked,* or *unclear,* in order to create a sense of urgency and to set the tone.

Headline: What's something great you've done that can reinforce why you are here and demonstrate your expertise? Don't shy away from using key words that resonate with your audience.

Body: What can you share to back up your bold headline? This can include facts, data, and examples. The body will confirm that you know what you're talking about.

Takeaway: How can you end your statement so you're letting them know what you can offer? The easiest thing is to tease what you want to talk about.

The keys to a successful elevator pitch are: it should be succinct and not feel pushy or sales-y. A great elevator pitch is meant to be a catalyst for more conversation, because it's just enough to kick off the conversation. Being proud of your work, knowing it matters, and tailoring your message to what others care about is how you can stand out in a Loud Culture workplace. I have found that those who know the impact of their work build their credibility quickly and make a lasting impression.

Loud in a Quiet Culture

Christina Tess is a no-nonsense straight shooter, and she sees herself as someone who was raised with Loud Culture values. Spend a few minutes with her and you know she loves talking about her work and jumping into lively discussions. She also isn't shy about telling you what she wants. Working in New York City, she loved her office's Loud Culture vibe, because everything about it matched her own style of engagement. It even helped her rise up quickly in the corporate world, because she seamlessly built her credibility and career brand as a go-getter. But seven years in, Christina found herself needing to move to California for personal reasons. So she got a new job running the operations for a top-tier investment firm in Silicon Valley.

"People at this company say I am really intimidating

and abrasive when I speak," said Christina as we jumped on our first call together. "I want people to feel comfortable around me, and I want to feel comfortable around them too."

Less than a year into working at her new firm, Christina said she began to feel that her Loud Culture traits, which had worked well for her in her Big Apple office, were turning people off in her San Francisco office. In this new environment, she said many of her colleagues displayed more Quiet Culture behaviors, so when she would excitedly jump into a conversation, she'd unintentionally bulldoze the discussion. Or when she spoke up, her tone would sound very loud and accusatory, which didn't create the feeling that others were invited to the conversation.

Christina said she didn't want to come off this way, but her communication style, she realized, was having a negative effect on her team and hurting people's perception of her.

Unlike most of the clients I work with, Christina wanted help rethinking her Loud Culture values among her Quiet Culture team. It wasn't about having her embody Quiet Culture traits, which would have felt inauthentic to who she was. Instead, it was about her leaning in to the Cultural Reframes, specifically Engage Others, so she could focus on her audience and the people in the room, not just what she wanted to say.

Over the next several weeks, we worked on how

she could be more conscientious when relating to her colleagues in meetings, including reading the room. We talked about how she could thoughtfully insert herself into a conversation without making others feel like their ideas were less important, and being mindful of her tone. (We talk more about tone of voice in part 3.)

Over time, using the Cultural Reframes, Christina went from challenging and debating in a seemingly abrasive way to thinking about others and what was important to them, and adjusted her tone accordingly. This completely transformed how she engaged with her Quiet Culture team. Because it wasn't about not contributing her thoughts, it was about rethinking the way she did it under the cultural context she was now operating in.

"I feel much more confident walking into meetings now," said Christina after a few months of us working together. "I used to feel confused as to how to act, but now I see reading the room and chiming in at the right time allows me to be seen as a thoughtful team player in this particular environment."

Once Christina realized that the friction she was experiencing was simply a misalignment of expectations, she felt a huge sense of relief. The Cultural Reframes helped her articulate her thoughts in a more well-rounded way, which caused people to be more receptive to her suggestions. As a result, the credibility she had easily built in a Loud Culture was now also achievable among her Quiet Culture peers.

WORD TO THE WISE

 Establishing our credibility is a never-ending process. The key is to always get a temperature check of who is around us and what they care about. Observe the dynamic of the room and look for verbal and nonverbal cues. This will ensure we are presenting ourselves in the best way possible, because doing otherwise can jeopardize the credibility we want to build.

THE BOTTOM LINE

- Building credibility is the second step of our Quiet Capital Framework.

- In a Quiet Culture, credibility is often attributed to age and hierarchical levels.

- In a Loud Culture, credibility is earned and re-earned, and it is the product of respect and trust.

- Respect is gained through the actions we take.

- Trust is built through what we say.

- Communicating what's going on, especially when things don't go as planned, can make the difference between protecting and shattering our workplace credibility.

- The TACT Framework is a way of structuring our message so it's clear and intentional: **T**ake a moment, **A**rticulate the process, **C**ommunicate solutions, **T**alk it out together.

- A strong elevator pitch entails saying just enough so others want to know more.

CHAPTER 6

ADVOCATING FOR OURSELVES

Getting what we want

My heart was racing a mile a minute and my hands were tightly wrapped around my cell phone. I was about to call my boss to ask for something I had been hoping for: to fill-in anchor. As a young TV reporter, I had dreamed of one day anchoring an entire newscast, because for many of us in the industry, this was considered the most distinguished role. It meant you were now the "face" of a TV station and you had the finesse and expertise to command the attention of viewers. But at this point, I had only practiced anchoring behind the scenes. I leaned on the generosity of my colleagues who stayed late after work to help me practice reading the teleprompter so I could record a sample video of my work. Not surprisingly, the more I practiced it, the more I wanted to do it. But I knew I wasn't alone. Most of my peers wanted this coveted opportunity too. And for months, I saw them each get it.

How did they get it? Did my boss just offer it to them? Did they deserve it more than I did? These were some of the questions and doubts that ran through my head. But deep down, I knew the answer—at minimum, they got what they wanted because they asked for it. And more important, they were persistent about it.

When we think about the things we want, whether personal or professional, what are some of the reasons why we hold ourselves back and don't ask for them? Or maybe we do muster up the courage to ask, but we wonder, is asking once enough? Remember my story of when the Thunderbirds, the US Air Force Air Demonstration Squadron, came into town and I raised my hand to cover the story, only to get sidelined? Or when Kevin, the junior associate who was expecting a promotion because he worked hard, was passed over for it? Both stories highlight how so many of us raised with Quiet Culture traits think either asking once is enough or that working hard alone will get us there.

However, we now know that getting what we want requires a mindset shift, and requires action. Here, we move into the third and final pillar of our Quiet Capital Framework: advocating for ourselves. We will take all that we've learned from shaping our career brand and building credibility to now ask for the things we want. We will also dive into how to follow up, showcase our wins, and get comfortable saying no. In essence, we will learn how to **A**sk, **C**ircle back, **C**elebrate, and **T**urn down work when needed. These actions, which I call ACCT, are how we can effectively stand up for ourselves and act on behalf of our interests. Because in a Loud Culture working world, we can't expect others to advocate for us. We have to get good at finding and creating opportunities for ourselves, and we have to proactively integrate this into our everyday work.

Here is ACCT at a glance:

- **A: Ask** for what we want
- **C: Circle back** to stay top of mind
- **C: Celebrate** our wins
- **T: Turn down** requests

Keeping these four practices in mind and learning how to do them effectively will help us speak up and stand up for ourselves. Because right now, while we may know these things are important to do, because of our Quiet Culture values we may not know *how* to do them, so we end up not doing them at all, or executing them haphazardly. In this chapter, we will go over each of these four areas in detail so you will know what to say and how to say it whenever you need to advocate for yourself at work.

ASK: GET OTHERS TO SEE THE VALUE OF YOUR REQUEST

Let's go back to the story I started the chapter with, the moment I was about to call my boss and ask to fill-in anchor. With the phone ringing, I suddenly heard his voice come on the other end. "Hi, Nathan!" I said in my most cheerful tone. "Thanks for taking the time to chat with me. So, I wanted to ask, I have been thinking about anchoring for a while now and I'd like the opportunity to potentially fill-in anchor, maybe sometime over the weekend if there is a spot," I said.

Silence.

"Well," my boss finally responded. "There are a lot of people we are rotating through right now, but I will keep you in mind."

"Oh, OK, great, thanks! I appreciate you taking the time," I said, and hung up quicker than I could even say goodbye.

As the call ended, I felt a mix of relief and restlessness. For one, I gave myself a pat on the back for finding the courage to ask for what I wanted. But I also felt like I didn't do a good job of actually asking for it. I didn't even give myself the chance to explain why I was interested; it was like a fog rolled through my brain, and I wanted to get out of that situation as fast as I could. In that moment, I knew I had to get better at asking for things, because there were surely going to be more moments like this in the future.

For those of us who come from a Quiet Culture, asking for what we want can feel challenging because it is not in our nature to communicate in such a direct and explicit way. In the communications world, we say that communicating is either low-context or high-context, a concept developed by anthropologist Edward Hall. In low-context communication, people share their thoughts by engaging in more direct messaging and saying exactly what they mean; it's interpreted literally. Essentially, this means "Tell them what you are going to tell them, then tell them what you've told them." Here's an example of a direct ask: "Please update the Excel spreadsheet, because there is an error on page four. The numbers do not match the data. Please give me the corrected version by five p.m. today." While blunt, there is no obscurity in this messaging, and it conveys the request in a direct way.

However, in high-context communication, people speak more indirectly, and messages are implied. For those who communicate this way, the assumption is that other people will understand, even though the ask wasn't explicitly laid out. For instance, an indirect ask could be, "I took a look at the Excel spreadsheet, and some parts might be confusing to others. You might want to check the data if you have time, and if you're able to, please get it back to me, maybe sometime today?" You can see that in high-context speaking, the ask is more subtle, and the deadline can even be misconstrued as flexible. A person who understands high-context communication, though, will be able to read between the lines and know that while it wasn't directly made, the request wasn't any less important. In my own experience and from years of observing workplace communication, I've discovered that people who come from Quiet Cultures tend to ask for things in a high-context way, either because they were told it was the polite thing to do or because it will come off less forcefully. This is important to keep in mind because when we work in a Loud Culture environment, low-context communication is generally expected.

The moment I hung up the phone with my manager, I knew I had to be more deliberate—low-context—with my ask. Fortunately, I didn't have to look very far. I could leverage a communication technique many of my veteran colleagues used in the office, and I could emulate them to be more convincing. They deftly used the Cultural Reframe of Engage Others, and they embodied keeping their audience in mind in their storytelling pitch. Watching their pitches felt like a lesson in effective speaking, and it helped me refine mine as well.

So how did they do it? They always started their ask by explaining the timeliness of their idea and why people should care. They framed their request by talking about how it would benefit their stakeholder (the producer), including letting them know if it would give them an exclusive, or any sort of competitive advantage. This framing, which put their stakeholder at the center of their message, was what made their ask compelling, because the producers could now see the benefits quickly. It was no surprise that these veteran reporters almost always got their stories picked up: they could talk about the things their audience cared about.

How can you apply this same approach when asking for what you want? Over time, I was able to see it in three steps:

1. Make a strong case
2. Align objectives
3. Explain why you're the one asking for it

To crystallize what to say in each part, answer the questions in the following table.

OBJECTIVE	QUESTIONS TO ANSWER
Make a strong case	• Why now? • Who will it benefit and why? • Any numbers or data to support your claim?
Align objectives	• What do your stakeholders care about? • Will it cost money, time, or resources, and where would that come from? • Is the ROI worth it for the organization or team?
Explain why you're the one asking for it	• Why are you the right fit for this? • Why do you want to do it?

Asking for what we want is always about putting others at the center of our request. It's about asking the right questions so we can anticipate our audiences' needs and know exactly how to respond. Because many times, when we ask for something, we only have minutes to make an impression. If others don't see the value of it, or they pose a question we don't have the answers to, they may dismiss our request altogether. Being strategic can ensure we're framing our communication in a straightforward and low-context way, while still getting our point across.

Back to my request to fill-in anchor on TV. A few months passed, and I still wasn't being called from the sidelines. As uncomfortable as it was, the voice in my head was telling me I needed to revisit the conversation with my manager. One day as he and I were wrapping up a discussion on another topic, I casually brought up the opportunity to fill-in anchor again, but this time I took the answers I had carefully brainstormed and embedded them into my request so it was more tailored, direct, and clear.

"Also, I wanted to see again if there were any future opportunities for me to fill-in anchor," I began. "I know the main anchor may be out on vacation or sick sometimes, so if that happens, I am happy to come in and help, even on my day off. Don't worry, I'm happy to do this on top of my regular duties. I have done a lot of practice rounds, which you can see in the recordings I sent you a few weeks ago."

Two things happened here. I completely reconfigured my message *and* I reminded my boss of my request. The **strong** case was pointing out real-life scenarios when spots might open; **aligning** objectives was calling out what was likely on his mind—whether this opportunity would prevent me from finishing my regular duties—and giving an answer. And **explaining why** I was asking for it, which was about my interest, commitment, and dedication. Compared to my initial request, this execution felt much more substantial and clear.

"Thanks for reminding me," Nathan replied. "I'll take a look at the video and the schedule."

Whew, I thought. My manager's response was so casual, it was a reminder that sometimes the anxiety surrounding what we want is loudest in our own head.

A few weeks later, I found myself in the anchor seat, and I

couldn't be more thrilled to have had the courage to advocate for myself.

For those of us raised with Quiet Culture values, it's especially easy to put our own desires aside because we want to be mindful of others. While that *is* part of being a good communicator, doing so to the point that we mute our own desires is when it starts to hurt us, not help us. So think of it this way: We ask for what we want because we care about it. We just need to make sure others care about it too. We should not let our fear of rejection prevent us from asking for the things we want. In fact, we shouldn't see "no" as case closed. Instead, we should see it as a redirect, in which we just have to find another way to circle back.

CIRCLE BACK: REPEATED ATTEMPTS WILL BE NECESSARY

For some of us, just asking for what we want is hard enough. Add to that the need to circle back and it can feel downright overwhelming. To overcome the mental hurdle of following up, we have to realize that we are often our own harshest critic. The fear, rejection, embarrassment, guilt, and even shame we may feel, while very much real, are often made much worse by our negative self-talk. Just like we discussed with the Journalist's Approach in chapter 3, we have to give ourselves the space to question whether an initial no is the end of the conversation or whether we're *assuming* it's the end of the conversation. In fact, it's helpful to point out the reality of our fears versus the actual perception people have of us. I like to run the following exercise, in which I compare my fears to the optimistic possibilities of people's reactions.

YOUR FEARS	THEIR REACTION
I already asked once and I don't want to be seen as pushy.	I hear you, I just need time to think about it. I am glad you reminded me.
I don't want to ask for help again because it'll be a sign of weakness.	I appreciate you taking the initiative. This discussion will help us avoid bigger problems later.
I don't want to ask for more because I don't want to appear greedy.	I can tell you're interested in this. If it's well justified, I will consider it.
I don't want to ask for feedback because it might bother people.	I can tell you care about this. You want to make things better.

Seeing this laid out side by side helps reduce the fear that often comes with circling back. While each one of these fears is valid, the reaction may not be as negative as we think. In fact, researchers have a name for people who don't take that additional step to follow up and instead just let things be: prevention-focused. These are people who tend to operate on the safe side, and they prefer not to disturb the status quo. Prevention-focused people are motivated by not losing what they already have. They feel it's OK to ask just once and assume that's enough. This tends to resonate with those from a Quiet Culture. We sometimes let things be and wait for opportunities to come to us instead of seeking them out.

On the flip side, those from a Loud Culture will often gun for what they want, and they'll do it openly and regularly. Researchers call these people promotion-focused, and they play to *win*. They see their goal as a path to gain some sort of reward. They put themselves out there and ask for what they want, and they feel a reward unearned is a failure to advance.

Researchers have found that depending on our motivation style, we can actually push ourselves by reframing our mindset. For example, one study divided soccer players into prevention-focused and promotion-focused groups, and they were coached based on their style. Promotion-focused players were told, "You are going to shoot five penalties. Your aspiration is to score at least three times," while prevention-focused players were told, "You are going to shoot five penalties. Your obligation is to not miss more than twice." The research found that when the participants were coached based on their motivational style, their performance improved significantly. This was especially true for the prevention-focused players, who scored nearly twice as often when they heard the "don't miss" instructions.

For those of us from Quiet Cultures, this bit of insight can be helpful. If we are prevention-focused, then we can think about what we might lose if we don't follow up. To get on that next big project, create our own project, or just have a seat at the table, we need to think about the opportunities we might not get because we asked just once. In fact, acknowledging that sometimes a no isn't the end of the conversation can help. We need to think maybe the other person just needs time to process what we've said.

There is also a practical side to circling back. According to researchers, people often underestimate how many times they need to say something for their message to stick. Harvard Business professor John Kotter once wrote that companies undercommunicate what they want by at least a factor of ten. That is a huge difference, especially if it's something we want. Now, does this mean we ask for something the same way multiple times? Well, no, because doing that would turn off anyone we're talking to. The key is to find alternate ways of addressing what we're asking for.

This is where thinking about how we circle back can give us the best fighting chance to get that eventual yes. Similar to asking for what we want, our circling back should be carefully crafted to bolster our case, especially if our idea was not met with initial excitement or resounding approval. So, when circling back, we have to think about our content, platform, and timing to ensure we are catching people at the right moment and to move the conversation forward. Let's look at these three areas more closely so we can strengthen our follow-up approach.

1. **Content**
   - We made our point the first time. What can we now show that will match our words with our intent?

- What new behaviors can we exhibit to drive our point forward?
- Is there another angle we can take?

2. **Platform**
   - How did we communicate our message the first time, and how can we do it differently next time? If it was through email, maybe try following up another way—in person or via phone, text, or video calls.
   - How can we communicate indirectly? For example, whom can we chat with who might not be directly impacted by our request, but still holds influence?

3. **Timing**
   - When did we first reach out, and when is another possible time? (Be specific!) Consider following up on a different day at a different time and when they are in a different headspace.
   - How long has it been since we last followed up? Leave enough time between the initial ask and the follow-up, but don't wait too long, or else the other side might not remember at all. A sweet spot is about a week, unless it is urgent or timely.

The power of going through this sequence of questions is that it helps us brainstorm what to do next, while redirecting any feelings of disappointment. Oftentimes, when we hear that hesitation or initial no, we may take it personally, dwell, or worse yet, think it's case closed. Instead, we have to treat the follow-up as if it's an expected part of the process. Here's a real-life example of taking content, platform, and timing into consideration and applying them to how we circle back. In chapter 4, I talked about shaping our career brands, and I mentioned the time I wanted to create a career brand for myself as a business journalist. To ensure I was exercising my intangible skills, I conceptualized, created, and pitched a business show. However, what I didn't mention was that this idea was rejected a few times before coming to fruition. I had to continually follow up with my manager to keep it a top priority. But because this project was something I cared about and believed in, I found there was no other choice but to focus on what I might lose if I didn't keep trying.

So to prepare, I thought about how I would broach the subject again. I have found that when circling back, it's best to start the conversation in a more casual and friendly tone. The reason is because when we are reminding someone of something, we don't want to force them to make a decision when they're not ready. For example, a serious tone could signal impatience and a lack of consideration of their time. The opening sentences that follow are a great way to keep the conversation flowing without putting too much pressure on the other to make a decision. Consider these conversation starters:

- *"Hi, ____, do you have a few minutes?"*
- *"Also, I've been thinking about ____, and wanted to quickly share what else I came up with."*
- *"By the way, did you have a chance to review ____?"*

Now, with the conversation opened, here's how I used the checklist of questions to revisit my business show request:

CONTENT

- We made our point the first time. What can we **show** that'll match our words with our intent?

  I shared a branding sheet with business show names to help my manager visualize what this program could be, so it felt real.

- What new **behaviors** can we exhibit to drive our point forward?

  I showed tenacity and dedication by saying, "I've also been researching what else is on the market . . ."

- Is there another **angle** we can take?

  Instead of talking about why now, I angled the benefit by talking about how there was nothing like this in the market and we would be the first to launch this unique show.

PLATFORM

- How did we first communicate our message to the other person, and how can we do it **differently** next time?

  The first follow-up was in person, and the subsequent follow-up was through email with new materials attached.

- How can we communicate **indirectly**?

  I connected with my assistant producer who I knew could vouch for my idea.

TIMING

- When did we first reach out, and when could be **another time**?

  The first follow-up was a Thursday afternoon after lunch, and the second was the following Friday morning after our editorial meeting.

- **How long** has it been since we last followed up?

  There was about a week and a half in between each follow-up.

In total, it took following up two more times after the initial ask before I got the final yes from my manager. Did it feel awkward? Yes. Did I think about giving up? Yes. Was it worth it in the end? *Yes.* Seeing the words *Hudson Valley Business Beat* come on the TV screen was a victory, both personally and professionally. On my résumé, I could now write "launched the first-ever business show in the local market." But even more important, I was advocating for myself, keeping it top of mind, and I could not have been more proud.

CELEBRATE: OUR WINS ARE WORTH HIGHLIGHTING

When something great happens to you at work (you finish a tedious project, you meet your key performance indicators, you close a new client), how do you celebrate? You are probably feeling pretty happy and proud, and that initial rush of excitement gets you thinking about the kinds of opportunities it might unlock. But just as quickly as that happy energy washed over you, self-doubt and panic may also set in. Unwelcome thoughts like, *Was it just luck? Will that win ever happen again?* may start to flood your mind.

Chances are, you're doing incredible work, and really, you deserve much more credit than you give yourself. For people raised in Quiet Cultures, working hard comes naturally. We are reliable and hardworking, and we take our projects and deadlines seriously. But if we want to advocate for ourselves and keep ourselves front and center for bigger opportunities, we have to get comfortable not just doing the work but also talking about our work. Earlier in the book, we talked about the Cultural Reframe for how we Handle Wins and how we need to showcase how it benefits the greater good. This is the section where we give that reframe actionable steps so people can notice our efforts, without going against our nature of being humble or modest. Because while showcasing our wins does require us to sometimes make the first move, it doesn't mean we can't do it in a way that feels right. Here's a story to show you how to think about this.

It was a typical workday for us reporters and producers at ABC 10News in San Diego. As we were filing into our morning meeting, my manager walked into the room with an intense look on her face. She had just finished watching a viral video, and she wanted us to cover what was happening. A man in San Diego had built a gigantic truck and was driving it recklessly around the streets, jumping over bushes, doing wheelies in parking lots, and creating a lot of ruckus. The stunt was recorded on video, and, not surprisingly, it was being shared at lightning speed. My manager wanted us to find this driver and interview him so we could get his side of the story, because while social media loved it, his neighbors hated it.

"Jessica, we're going to assign you this story. We need you to find and talk to this driver," my boss said. I could see the excitement and determination on her face.

"Oh, OK, I'll try my best," I replied, trying to hide the uncertainty in my tone.

Without much to go on, I walked back to my desk and scoured the web. How in the world was I going to find, contact, and convince this total stranger on social media to talk to me on TV, all within the next few hours?

Surprisingly, after about an hour of searching online, I found the driver's contact information. I messaged him on Facebook and asked if he was willing to be interviewed. To my complete shock, he said yes. I jumped in the car, drove to his place, and conducted the interview in his kitchen.

As I drove back to the office with the interview secured, I celebrated in my head what a win this was. I knew my manager wanted this story badly, so to get it was a major victory. Now, the Quiet Culture part of me wanted to shrug off the accomplishment and say it was no big deal. But I knew that because I worked in a Loud Culture, this was an opportune time to showcase my win. Emphasizing it to her would ensure it wouldn't get lost in a sea of other assignments. So I leaned in to my

Handle Wins Cultural Reframe and walked straight to her office to talk about how this was a big win for the team.

"How'd it go?" my manager asked as I popped my head into her office.

"We just got our top story of the day!" I declared, beaming. "The driver spoke to us on camera and it's an exclusive interview. He shared so much; this is going to be a great story!"

In the world of news, exclusivity is a badge of honor. Immediately, a huge smile appeared on my manager's face. She responded with a slew of questions, including asking how I had done it and what the driver said. Together, we chatted about this accomplishment and what a win it was for the station. While this conversation was no more than two minutes, she decided then and there it was going to be our top story of the newscast.

This story has stuck with me, because what happened next cemented why celebrating our wins can be so important. A few days after the story aired, an email was sent out to the entire newsroom, including the highest level of management, praising the story and my effort. Suddenly, those who didn't even know me knew what I had done and the impact it had. The visibility from this one story was immeasurable.

So, how can you find opportunities to talk about your wins, especially if you know they're worth noting? Because at this point, we know it's not necessarily how much work we do, it's how we are using the work to build more visibility for ourselves. If this conjures up feelings from how we reframed Spend Time, you're right! It's about taking the great work we're doing and maximizing the opportunity so others know about it. In the working world, strategic placement of ourselves and our efforts is how we can set ourselves up for that next-level promotion. In fact, if you are nearing performance-review season, subtly dropping wins over the two to three months prior to your one-on-one meeting with your manager can prime them to see you are doing incredible work, which you are.

So how can we talk about our wins when our Quiet Culture instinct is to deflect or avoid it? Similar to asking for what we want, it helps to structure our message by thinking about the greater benefit, what steps we took, and to communicate it using "power words." By answering these questions, we can get a better idea of what to say when talking about our work.

1. Articulate the benefit
   - How did our accomplishments help **others**? Why did it matter to them?

2. Be open about the process
   - What **steps** did we take to accomplish this task? State one to three points.

3. Communicate using power words
   - What **emotions** did we feel with this win? Use words like *excited, happy, proud.*

Articulating the benefit is how we can capture our listeners' attention because they'll know what's in it for them. Being open about the process is how we can talk about what we did so others appreciate the effort. Communicating using power words is expressing our enthusiasm with strategic words so others get excited about it too. Here are some examples of what this could sound like with all three elements addressed:

SCENARIO: You finished putting together an Excel spreadsheet for the team.

SCRIPT: "I wanted to share how much easier it'll be for us to sift through the data now. You can see I've placed everything into these tabs, which I organized in numerical order. I'm pretty excited about how much time this will save us!"

SCENARIO: You finished redesigning the marketing collateral.

SCRIPT: "I'm sending over this folder of our new set of marketing collateral. I changed the font, adjusted the color, and even added a few more pictures. I think these look so much better!"

SCENARIO: You closed a new client or customer.

SCRIPT: "I can't wait to start working with ABC company. I just spoke with them over the phone and went over XYZ, so they know what's coming. It's going to be great!"

Remember, advocating for ourselves doesn't require us to be loud or brash. It is simply standing up for things we are proud of.

It's knowing that our work, effort, and impact matter. How we might have internalized Handle Wins before must be readjusted so we feel pride in our work every day, even though we might not feel it's 100 percent perfect. It also requires remembering that celebrating our wins can be short and sweet. Because as my mom would say, if we're not our own cheerleader, who will be?

Good News Is Always Worth Sharing

Sarah Branson was a promising young employee at her boutique public relations firm. A few years out of college, she was already getting media placements for her clients at top-tier outlets like *The New York Times* and *Today*. Part of her success was due to her ability to build relationships with both her clients and the media, so it was a win-win opportunity for both sides. But there was one problem. Sarah said that while she was great at getting her job done, she was having trouble building a good relationship with her manager.

"I feel like every time I talk to my boss now, it's just transactional," she said. "We only talk to each other if I need something from her or if she needs something from me."

Sarah said she couldn't pinpoint why or how this had come to be, but every time they conversed, it was cold and curt. If there were others in the room, her boss would direct her attention to them and not her. Sarah said she didn't want this lack of interpersonal connection to be a reason why she jumped ship to find another job. And while she knew she didn't have to be friends with her manager, she at least wanted to develop more rapport in the workplace. So Sarah decided to do her best to solve the problem as if her job depended on it.

One of the first things we worked on was taking her strength—building relationships with her clients and people in the media—and seeing if she could apply the same approach with her manager. So I asked her about her approach.

"It's a careful balance so they remember me, because I can't always reach out with requests; otherwise I'll come off as too pushy. But I also have to stay in touch," Sarah explained. "I guess every time I do talk to the media, I make it relevant and timely to the things they care about."

"Whatever you're doing with the media, you've got to do with your manager too," I responded.

We then discussed how she could find things to talk about with her manager that didn't seem abrupt or out of the blue. We outlined a list of wins that she could regularly share with her boss, including grabbing a physical copy of a newspaper to showcase her placements. It didn't have to be in a loud or ostentatious way, just a small and proactive "wanted to send this to you" or "check this out," so her manager could see what was going on for *their* clients, which she knew her manager cared about too.

A few weeks later, Sarah reported that while the first few interactions felt stiff, through time, it got easier. She said she noticed her boss softening the more she casually popped into her office, and their engagements became less transactional and more conversational.

WORD TO THE WISE

 Create a folder in your email labeled "Yay Folder," and drop in any emails in which people are congratulating or acknowledging your contributions, big or small. This Yay Folder is your go-to if you ever need evidence showcasing your good work. It's also a great place to search for examples if you ever need a confidence boost at work!

TURN DOWN: CREATE BOUNDARIES AND SET EXPECTATIONS

Part of advocating for ourselves is learning how to confidently and gracefully say no. For many of us raised with Quiet Culture values, it's easier to acquiesce and accept projects because we want to be seen as a team player. But in the process of always saying yes, we sacrifice our time and take on work that does not really help us. While accepting projects and being a team player is critical to being well-liked and respected at work, saying yes out of fear can hurt us.

Early on as a reporter, I struggled a lot with saying no. I felt like it was easier to say yes, and if someone was more senior than I was, I didn't think I even had the option of saying no because of the power distance. This explained why, when I started working in a Loud Culture, I was floored to see some of my colleagues turn down work, both from my manager and for projects they were assigned to do. It was counterintuitive to everything I was taught. But I realized that if I wanted to be noticed and not be mistaken for just a quiet hard worker, I needed to learn how to confidently and respectfully say no.

To lean in to strategically saying no, I studied how some of the most seasoned reporters confidently debated and challenged each other and my manager in meetings. I observed how they framed their *no* and how they followed up if others pushed back. While this kind of exchange didn't happen all the time, it happened enough to see there was both a structure and an art to it. In fact, the seasoned reporters leaned in to a communication technique I already knew but wasn't yet using myself.

Our job as journalists is to go out and interview people and hold them accountable for their actions. There are often tricky conversations with politicians, business executives, or even everyday people who are doing things with public consequences. And while these conversations are often uncomfortable, as journalists, we are tasked with walking the fine line of pushing delicately (so the subject won't close up) yet communicating firmly (so we can still get the answers we need). To achieve this balance, practicing the highest level of social and self-awareness is critical. For example, being mindful of our tone, giving a brief explanation, and following up with options are some of the subtleties that can make the difference between breaking a relationship and building mutual understanding. This exact formula can actually be summed up as TEF, which is short for Tone, Explain, and Follow. Let's run through each so we know how they can be applied at work.

T: Tone is the overarching driver, affecting our delivery and how people perceive our message. When we say no, we have to be mindful of keeping our tone of voice neutral and matter-of-fact, so others feel our certainty.

E: Explain and share why we're saying no so others don't feel like we're dismissing them. For example, we're currently up on a deadline, our workload can't handle any additional duties, or we're not the right person for this.

F: Follow with options because it shows we still care and we don't want to leave them hanging. For example, we can suggest alternative times for others to check in when we have more free time, or provide other avenues for them to explore.

TONE

EXPLAIN	**FOLLOW**

Here are two sample scripts of turning down requests confidently and diplomatically:

"Thanks for thinking of me, but I won't be able to help with X project right now. I currently have a large deadline. However, reach out to me again next Friday, because I should be freer then."

"This sounds like an interesting idea, but I don't think I'm the right one for it. It's actually not something I'm familiar with, but I suggest you check out ABC; they may have some resources."

While turning down a request can feel daunting, keeping in mind our tone, giving a short explanation, and following up with options can help us feel more confident in our approach. This structure also strikes a balance, allowing us to kindly and clearly get our thoughts across while not making people feel like we don't care or we're disrespecting them. Because in saying no, we are still helping people in other ways, including providing *other* options that might actually be better. Above all, saying no ensures we are creating boundaries for ourselves and we're holding them in place; because in the working world, people tend to respect those who stand their ground. It's not selfish, it's smart.

IN THE END, whether we are asking for what we want, circling back, celebrating our wins, or turning down a request, we need to ACCT on behalf of our best interests at work. Advocating for ourselves is one of the three pillars that form our Quiet Capital Framework, because while our Cultural Reframes help us rethink our approach to the workplace, our Quiet Capital Framework gets us the recognition we deserve. In fact, as people raised with Quiet Culture values, we have to get into the mindset that these three pillars of the Quiet Capital Framework are not just "good to do," they're a "must do." When we know what our career brand is, build credibility, and advocate for ourselves, others will see that we indeed have our own thoughts, needs, and aspirations. More important, it's how we can ensure we're being noticed for all the right reasons.

THE BOTTOM LINE

- Relying on others to hand us opportunities will just lead to disappointment and frustration. We have to be our own best advocate.

- When at work, we need to ACCT in our own best interests.

- **Ask** for what we want by building a strong case, aligning our objectives, and explaining why we're the best person for the job. Keeping these elements in mind can help others see the value of our request.

- **Circle back** to stay top of mind by considering the content, platform, and timing. These three elements can help us gauge how and when to make that ask again, because repeated attempts will be necessary.

- **Celebrate** our wins by articulating the benefit, being open about the process, and communicating using power words. It's how others can see what we're doing and why it matters.

- **Turn down** requests by thinking about our tone, explaining why, and following up with options, because saying no is how we create boundaries and set expectations.

PART 3

THE COMMUNICATION ADVANTAGE

One of the biggest misconceptions about work is that as long as we do good work, others will notice it. However, we now know that if we want to be noticed exactly the way we want to be, we have to be strategic about it. That's why in part 3, we will dive into developing our communication skills and go over these skills in detail. We will focus on the three main tools that make up our communication toolbox: our words, our tone, and our body language. Because when we marry strategic communication skills with the work we do, our competitive advantage becomes undeniable. People will notice and remember us, and we will see the biggest opportunities start to unfold.

CHAPTER 7

MAXIMIZING OUR WORDS

What we say speaks volumes

Two weeks before Christmas 2021, I found the following email in my inbox:

> I'm a first-generation immigrant from China and I'm currently working in private equity in North America. I need to come off as very polished and "alpha male" confident.

In just these two sentences I could feel both a sense of urgency and desperation. Sarah Lin was having a Quiet Culture versus Loud Culture crisis. Growing up in China, Lin gravitated toward traits associated with a Quiet Culture, but now that she was working in a Loud Culture global finance firm in the US, she was struggling: she thought she needed to act like an "alpha male" to be heard the way she wanted. She needed help improving her situation, so we quickly scheduled a meeting.

"I actually talk a lot in meetings," said Lin. "I always share my thoughts whenever they pop up."

"That's great," I replied. "So, where do you think the workplace friction comes from?"

"I think it's the way the conversation stops the moment I say something. Maybe I am overthinking it, but I don't think I speak up at the right time. I need better judgment on when to chime in."

Lin said that while she was being heard, she could tell it wasn't in a way that showcased her knowledge and expertise. Every time she spoke, she raised her voice to a loud, booming tone so everyone could hear her. She also spoke quickly to ensure other people did not cut her off. Yet despite doing everything she thought she was supposed to, she could feel the tension in the room. Her colleagues would just stare blankly at her with little to no response; they also didn't seem to add much of their own perspective to build on her contributions. It was clear that Lin needed to leverage her Cultural Reframes so she could better gauge what to communicate, and how to do so in a clear and discerning way.

The first thing we did was talk about the intersectional invisibility women of color face in the workplace. Acknowledging this helped her realize there was an added barrier to being seen the way she wanted to be. We talked about the Quiet Culture bias and how even though we can't always control the perception people have of us, we can be our own best advocate. I pointed out that she needed to eliminate the belief that she had to code-switch and act like an alpha male.

"The mark of an effective speaker isn't necessarily being the loudest one. What you need to do is think about *how* you speak," I said. "This can be achieved by thinking of your Cultural Reframe of Engage Others, which is to be mindful of your audience and tailor your message to the things they care about."

"But Jessica," Lin interjected. "I don't have enough data points to know what they care about, or when I should speak up and how I should interact."

It was an unexpected response, but I knew where Lin, an analytical-minded person, was coming from. The fact that she didn't have data or numbers to study made calculating the situation difficult. Without the data, she said she couldn't know if she was making the right judgment call to insert herself.

The truth is, Lin is a bit of an anomaly when it comes to the clients I typically work with. More often than not, my clients, most of whom were raised with Quiet Culture values, struggle with inserting themselves into a conversation at all. But regardless of whether speaking up feels seamless, being an effective communicator requires skill. In the following sections, we'll do a deep dive into how we can better speak and show up in various settings at work. Because if our Cultural Reframes give us a new way of approaching the workplace, our Quiet Capital Framework gives us the tools to apply it. Ultimately, it's our ability to effectively communicate that pulls it all together.

CONTRIBUTING IN MEETINGS

Finding the right words to say in front of others can be one of the most frustrating games we play in our own head. We can be sitting in a meeting quietly processing what's happening, while the other side of our brain is telling us loudly that we *have* to say something. Many of us raised in a Quiet Culture know that voice well—it's the voice that taunts us to say something before someone else says what we're thinking, and it's the voice that douses our confidence because we overanalyze the situation. The result is we either say something in an unclear or inelegant way, or we say nothing.

So how can we contribute in meetings and talk about our work, showcase our expertise, or advocate for ourselves when others are around? Instead of clamming up, we have to return to our Engage Others Cultural Reframe. Thinking about who is in the room and what they care about is the first step to ensuring our message is positioned for maximum impact.

After that, we need to execute with timing in mind and identify the opportune moment to insert ourselves; that is, the moment when people will be more receptive to what we're saying. If we disrupt the flow, others may feel we're being rude, thus turning off their willingness to hear us out. So, to effectively speak up in meetings, we need to become masters of timing to seamlessly introduce ourselves into a lively discussion. Here's a sequence of actions that can help us. It's called the 4A Sequence: **A**ctive listening, **A**cknowledging, **A**nchoring, and **A**nswering. This sequence is powerful because it gives us the exact rules and cues to look for that will help us identify when it is the right time to join in. Here's how it works:

ACTIVE LISTENING: Gauge Timing

Right now, when we hear the words *active listening*, giving feedback to help others may come to mind. We engage in active listening so we can better understand people and give them constructive feedback so they can improve. However, active listening in the context of contributing in meetings is different. We actively listen to gauge when it is the right time to insert ourselves into the conversation, especially when there are multiple people talking. For many of us, active listening comes easily, and we likely do it already. But instead of just listening for the sake of listening, we need to listen with the intent to speak. This switch is critical, because it tells our brain to listen for key words so we know when it is the right time to add our thoughts. For example, if the conversation has moved from talking about operations to talking about compliance, and we are part of that department, then now is the time to lean in to the conversation. Or if the team is talking about data and we sit on the data team, then now is the moment we laser in on what people are saying. More subtle cues to look for are things like body language and tone changes. For instance, someone may relax their posture and lean back, or they may start to look around—this is our cue to jump in. Or a change in vocal pitch can signal a thought is ending—our chance to begin speaking. Actively looking for these cues when listening is how we can get a temperature check of the situation. With timing defined, let's move on to adding ourselves into the conversation by acknowledging the person who spoke right before us.

ACKNOWLEDGING: Create Seamlessness

Once we've identified the right moment to speak up, the first few words out of our mouth should acknowledge what was just said. Acknowledging is a communication tactic that creates a seamless flow to the conversation. It also creates the impression we're there to collaborate, because we are recognizing others and their contributions too. If we jump into a conversation with phrases like, "Can I say something?" or "No, I don't agree," it can feel abrupt or even abrasive. Acknowledging is how we can create a more frictionless environment where people feel heard and are therefore more receptive to what we have to say. Here are examples of effective acknowledgments:

- *That's a really good point, Joyce; in fact . . .*
- *And if I may add to that, Carter . . .*
- *That's helpful to know, Max . . .*
- *Great idea, Kelly. It made me think of . . .*

By acknowledging the person before us, including saying their name, we put our active listening skills to use. To be clear, acknowledging isn't agreeing, it's just showing we're listening. In fact, if we do disagree, acknowledging is even more important, because we are inserting ourselves into the conversation without being too confrontational. For example, we can say:

- *That's an interesting point, Joyce. Have you thought about . . .*
- *I hear what you're saying, Carter; I am worried, though . . .*
- *I'm so glad you brought that up, Max. I had a concern about that . . .*
- *Thanks for sharing the information, Kelly. It makes me think . . .*

Once we've acknowledged the person before us, we will have gained the ears of those in the meeting. The next step is to anchor.

ANCHORING: Connect Points

In anchoring, we repeat one or two words spoken by the person we're listening to in order to maintain fluidity in the conversation. Anchoring is how we can connect what someone has said to what we want to say.

JOYCE: *The **financials** here don't look promising, so I think we need to go an entirely different direction.*

YOU: That's a good point you bring up, Joyce, the *financials* here . . .

CARTER: *The client thought the* **interface** *of our main page was hard to navigate.*

YOU: Thanks for sharing that, Carter, and I agree the *interface* can be improved, which is why we can consider . . .

MAX: *We spoke with the* **marketing department,** *and they had some corrections about the file we submitted.*

YOU: Yes, that's right, Max. The *marketing department* wasn't too excited about the XYZ proposal . . .

KELLY: *We can consider* **expanding** *our reach* **to the South Asia market.**

YOU: I hear what you're saying, Kelly. My concern with *expanding to the South Asia market* is we have yet to establish ourselves . . .

Anchoring is an effective technique because it challenges us to connect the dots between what someone said to what we want to say. It also reduces our use of filler words like *um* or *ah* because we are intentional with the point we want to make. With all eyes and ears on us, next, it's time to shine with our answer.

ANSWERING: Showcase Expertise

Everything we've discussed in the 4A Sequence can be executed in a matter of seconds. While the technique is quick, the impact is huge: we've now subtly prepared people to listen to us. It's here where we'll want to make our compelling point, suggestion, or pitch to showcase our expertise. However, I'd be remiss if I didn't say that this is where most people flub their opportunity to make a compelling point. Because with all eyes on them, many people get flustered and lose their train of thought. Or they may start mumbling or talking very fast. We've all seen it happen. So, how can we make sure we share our thoughts with clarity and conviction? We must ask ourselves what I call the golden question of communication: *What's the point I'm trying to make here?* It's a question so simple yet so powerful. On TV, journalists use it every day when formulating their message to sharpen their speaking. Here's a sequence to help you answer the golden question:

- **Make Your Point:** What you want them to know
- **Give Examples:** One or two thoughts explaining that point
- **Reiterate Your Point:** Restate your point to reinforce the message

That's it! Sometimes we can overcomplicate our answer when all we really have to do is sandwich our points together so people get it. It also helps us avoid talking in circles, especially if we're put on the spot. But if you ever find yourself being long-winded, just say, "What I'm trying to get at here is . . ."

Here is an example to illustrate the difference between a wordy message and a succinct message that both make exactly the same point.

Long-winded: There is a hospital in this city that is using a new innovative procedure to help those who have heart problems. It's pretty cutting-edge. The way the device works is that it's implanted into a person's body, and it dissolves after a period of time. Do you want to know what it is? [54 words]

Ask yourself: What's the point I'm trying to make here?

Punchy and Powerful: A local hospital unveiled a new cutting-edge heart procedure. It involves a device that dissolves inside patients. Want to hear more? [21 words]

Speaking up in meetings is about being pointed and succinct. It's also about considering nuances like timing, changes in body language, or a shift in tone, to make sure we're contributing at the right time. Using the 4A Sequence to determine when and how to insert ourselves into the conversation can make speaking up feel a lot smoother.

SPEAKING TO CONVINCE

Aristotle once said we speak to persuade, and it's the ultimate reason why we speak. In other words, at the heart of communicating effectively is our ability to convince others of our ideas. Many of us dream of one day becoming the kind of speaker who can move a crowd to action. Whether speaking to one, five, or five hundred people, we want to be the kind of communicator who can walk into a room, share our ideas, and have others feel inspired and motivated. That dream is not far off from being a reality as long as you know what to say and how to say it. In this section, we'll talk about how we can structure our communication to increase the chances of persuading others so they can see the brilliance of our ideas.

To begin, the ability to persuade is a learned skill for most of us. Many of the clients who come to me for communications help are brilliant in the technical space and can recite detailed jargon without breaking a sweat. But when it comes to eloquently expressing their thoughts and getting their team to act, things get tricky. They are uncomfortable with persuading because it feels pushy. Or when trying to convince someone who is perceived as higher status (such as a manager), they feel uncomfortable because it goes against their learned Quiet Culture value of deference. Persuading also means being more direct and explicit, which can be hard, especially if we prefer a more implicit style of communicating.

So, how can we speak to convince? When it comes to persuading others, we have to talk about using Persuasive Points and the Power of the Contrast, two strategies that can help us convince whomever we're speaking with at work.

Persuasive Points

Persuasive Points can be broken down into two categories: emotionally driven and quantitatively driven. Many of us use one or the other in our speaking already, but the real power is in using them together. Quantitatively driven points are facts, research, and numbers that back up our idea. Emotionally driven points are the feelings associated with those facts, and they give our words heart. When we marry both quantitatively and emotionally driven points together, we now speak to convince, because we are speaking to both the logical and emotional side of decision-making. This dual-faceted approach elevates our speaking.

Here are some examples of each type of point, along with examples of Persuasive Points, which is the combination of the two.

EMOTIONALLY DRIVEN POINTS	QUANTITATIVELY DRIVEN POINTS	PERSUASIVE POINTS
"We think you'll be missing out on this great opportunity to invest because we've been doing so well."	"Our sales numbers show ABC growth year over year, so investing now is ideal."	"Our numbers have been strong, and we're excited to show you why. If you look at our sales numbers year over year, you'll see ABC. So now would be an opportune time to consider investing."
"We've hit so many frustrating roadblocks with this software system that I think we need to pivot."	"We need to change because of all the problems we've hit: 1, 2, 3."	"It's been a tough month trying to fix this software system, and we've lost so much time and money. Here's what happened: 1, 2, 3. It's one thing after another, so I think it's time we consider something else."
"I've been working tirelessly this past quarter and want to ask for a raise."	"Here's everything I've done this past quarter, XYZ, to hit my performance metrics."	"I've been putting in the hours this past quarter, and I don't mind! However, I want to talk to you about a potential raise because I've done XYZ to hit my performance metrics and the impact has been huge for our team."

In the first two columns, we can see each makes a similar point, but the focus is on appealing to either the heart or the brain. The third column is where we combine them. By leveraging both the heart and the brain, we are creating Persuasive Points, effectively supercharging our speaking and making our point much more convincing. Here's another example of speaking with Persuasive Points.

Let's say you're trying to convince your marketing manager to invest in redesigning the company's old web page. It'll cost time and money, but you know it'll help with the page's conversion. So when speaking to convince, you can start by noting the friction points and the bounce rate, and then give numbers as proof to make your case stronger. Here's what you can say:

"Customers are visiting our web page, but we can tell there is a **problem**. They might be **confused** by all the buttons redirecting them to different places. We know this because customers don't click anything, and our bounce rate is **80 percent**. This is why I think we need to redesign our web page sooner rather than later."

By structuring your speaking using both emotionally driven and quantitatively driven points, you are appealing to your audience's heart *and* brain.

The Power of the Contrast

Just like Persuasive Points, the Power of the Contrast is a way of formulating your speech to convince. However, unlike

Persuasive Points, which leverages both the heart and brain to compel people to take action, the Power of the Contrast is a way of shaping your message so people can *understand* the impact of your idea quickly. Because when it comes to communicating in the workplace, even though you may know the benefit of your idea, if you don't highlight how challenging things are right now, others will feel only half the effect. This tip is best explained in the following table. The column on the left is the present and the column on the right is the future. In the left column, you'll note the pain points, gaps, or vulnerabilities of how things are right now, so others get a sense of the current situation. In the column on the right, for every challenge, you'll match it to a corresponding benefit or the impact your solution will provide. Think of it as parallels. For example, let's say you're explaining the benefit of your cybersecurity product to a prospective client. Instead of just focusing on the pain points or the benefits exclusively, you can use the Power of the Contrast to paint a complete picture.

CLIENT QUESTION:
How will this anti-piracy software help our company?

PRESENT: Most common vulnerabilities you see	FUTURE: How your product will protect against those vulnerabilities
$X million lost when hacked	$X million saved
What's not covered by other products	What's covered by your product

You can use the Power of the Contrast anytime you want to get others to understand the value of your idea. Because again, while you may know how useful your idea is, you can make your argument even stronger by sharing both the present and the future, which gives your idea depth.

Speaking to convince leverages both the heart and the brain. It also paints a picture by showing the present with the future to drive a point home. We can use one or both within the same conversation, but the point is to be intentional about it. When they are applied, we will no longer walk into a meeting and wonder if our points are convincing. They absolutely will be because we structured them to be so.

FILLER AND HEDGING WORDS

Ann Miura-Ko is the kind of person you read about and think, *She's got it all figured out.* She is a co-founding partner at Floodgate, a seed-stage venture capital firm, and she has invested in companies such as Lyft, Taskrabbit, and Refinery29. Forbes called her the "most powerful woman in startups," and *The New York Times* named her as one of the Top 20 Venture Capitalists Worldwide. She sits on the Board of Trustees for Yale University, her undergrad alma mater, just to round out her work experience. Yet despite her incredible accolades, Miura-Ko is quick to admit she struggled terribly with communicating early on.

"The way I was communicating created [an unintended perception] in the eyes of other people," she said as she reflected back on her early years of school.

While pursuing her PhD at Stanford University, Miura-Ko said she realized the way she was speaking was causing people to question her capabilities. Her communication was littered with filler words like *um, ah, uh, like, you know,* and so on.

Miura-Ko said this all came to a head one quarter when she was working on her senior thesis with her classmates. Their goal was to design autonomous soccer-playing robots. However, soon after they started, they ran into a problem and the robots weren't functioning the way they were supposed to. To troubleshoot, she said, each person had to explain what they were doing and what they were responsible for.

When it was her turn, Miura-Ko said her explanation was filled with words like *um* and *uh*, and it made her seem wavering and uncertain. Meanwhile, her teammates explained their side of the project with minimal filler words, which left the impression that they were confident and self-assured.

"They knew what I was capable of, and I knew what they were capable of. And yet there was that communication barrier, which created a lot of misgivings about what was happening within my area."

Miura-Ko said this experience showed her the power of the chosen word. "There is always an understood uncertainty about what you're reporting, and people know that," she said. "You don't have to reiterate it constantly [with *uhs, ums,* and *I think*]."

Regardless of where our overall communication skills fall right now, everyone has some level of filler words in their speaking. However, those of us raised with Quiet Culture values may find ourselves falling victim to them when we're in the spotlight, knee-deep in a contentious situation, or feeling self-conscious. Filler words sabotage our message, and they make us seem uncertain and even lacking in credibility. So if we want to talk about maximizing our words, we have to talk about reducing filler words. But how?

Eliminating filler words is about control. It's also trusting we know our material. Speaking slowly can allow us to think about our ideas and process what's going on at the same time. Controlling the speed of our talking gives us better rein of our own thoughts, because we are intentionally paying attention to the words that are coming out of our mouths, versus letting them go without thought. If you notice filler words creeping in, follow these steps to get them under control:

1. Pause
2. Breathe
3. Think
4. Speak with conviction

Reducing filler is that simple, yet we know it's incredibly hard to do. The key is to just keep trying. Catching yourself and pausing is the first step. The pause allows you to breathe and refocus. It also gives other people time to digest what you've said. In fact, researchers have studied the precise art of the pause and the effect it has on listeners. They found the most natural speeches include pauses that are 0.6 seconds within sentences, and either 0.6 seconds or 1.2 seconds between sentences. Research shows that intentional pauses can make speaking appear more natural for non-native English speakers too. While we won't have a timer to gauge our pauses in real life, it's enough to know pauses are good, and we should use them to speak with impact. Incorporating intentional pauses can improve how our message is perceived and received.

It's important to keep in mind that there will be moments when we'll need to *add* words that don't necessarily bring new insight to our ideas, but that are important to help round out our sentiment. These extra words are called hedging words, and they are valuable if we're not 100 percent sure of something, are trying to soften the blow of a contentious conversation, or are taking the edge off a harsh statement. It's especially important to use hedging words if we are thinking about our credibility, because we want to mean what we say. So if we are not sure of something, including phrases like "seems," "perhaps," "looks like," "not quite," "might," "basically," "I believe," and "well" can protect us so people don't use our words against us. Here are some examples:

- It *seems* like you're having a really rough day.
- *Perhaps* we need to look at the complaints.
- It *looks like* we're *not quite* agreeing on this.
- It *might* not be a good idea to do that.

Inserting hedging words is helpful when we're trying to get a temperature check of the situation. But above all, hedging words create a buffer and can protect our relationships and our reputation.

PRESENTING WITH EASE

You're in a meeting and the person presenting in front of everyone is noticeably nervous. You can tell because they're stiff as a board, their face is frozen in fear, and their speech is littered with awkward silences and filler words. As they're going through their slides, you are unsure what they're trying to say, because they can't get their point across clearly and effectively.

For most people, public speaking is no fun. As the popular saying goes, public speaking is feared more than death itself. And for many of us from a Quiet Culture, that fear resonates; we don't like putting ourselves in the spotlight, much less sharing our thoughts. We don't want our ideas to be brutally torn apart and we sure don't want to put our credibility on the line—what if we forget what we want to say and stand frozen like a block of ice? Not a good look.

But here's the thing about giving presentations—standing up and speaking in front of people will always feel a bit uncomfortable, regardless of how many times we do it. The nerves we feel may never fully go away, which some of the most seasoned public speakers will tell you is true. It's not a bad thing. Nerves and performance are actually closely linked. To achieve a high level of performance, we do need an optimal level of arousal (stress), because it can increase our alertness and our ability to act. Having no or too little stress can actually impede our performance. So the key is to know it, embrace it, and to use it to help us, not hurt us.

As a person who speaks in front of crowds of hundreds and even thousands, I'll admit, I still feel butterflies minutes before I go onstage. From the exterior it may not seem like it, but inside, the adrenaline and cortisol are coursing through my body. That's because every single speaking opportunity is different. The audience, the environment, and even the topic will vary depending on where I am. However, I've come to see that focusing on the message, not on the uncertainty, helps. Once I direct my attention from myself and toward how I am going to make my message resonate with the audience, I am able to focus on what actually matters: providing value. It's also helpful to remember that people watching are not there to witness me fail or fumble. They are there to learn. So as long as I know my material, believe it will help others, and frame it to show why people should care, everything else will fall into place.

It's why instead of asking ourselves how we can overcome the fear of public speaking, the better question is: How can we view the experience of giving presentations more constructively? There are three powerful mental shifts to keep in mind. First, think of presentations as conversations. We need to tell ourselves we're not speaking to a group; we're having a conversation with each person in the crowd, and we are just sharing what we know. We can further humanize the experience by reminding ourselves of the individuals in the room, rather than their titles: "I am speaking with Stephanie, not the senior vice president," or "I am speaking with Dan, not the prospective client." If we can humanize our audience, we can reduce the pressure we put on ourselves to be perfect.

The second mindset shift is to recognize that our audience doesn't know what we *intend* to say. They know only what we end up saying. That means when we miss a word or forget to make a point we wanted to make, our audience has no idea. We may feel missing a point was the worst thing that could've happened, but our audience knows only what they heard. So instead of getting flustered, feeling bad, or backtracking, we just need to keep going.

The third mental shift is to remind ourselves that speaking in front of others is putting our Cultural Reframe of Spend Time into action. Speaking in front of a group of people can be the most effective way to accelerate our career brand, build our credibility, and advocate for ourselves because we are reaching a large amount of people in a shorter amount of time. Maximizing every opportunity is ensuring people see us, hear us, and know what we're doing. Giving presentations is an excellent way to accomplish this because it positions us as experts, which can fast-track how we want to be seen.

So, embracing public speaking and finding opportunities to do it, perhaps starting in low-stakes situations, is how we can start to build our presentation muscle.

With a positive mindset in place, the next step is to figure out what we can say to appear clear and polished in front of a group of people. It goes without saying that preparation matters. But one of the best ways to convey confidence is using our transitions between slides to connect our points. If done right, it gives the impression that we know our stuff and we're a fluid speaker.

To hone this skill, let's talk about transition phrases and how we can use them to present with ease. Transition phrases can be divided into four categories: emphasizing, expanding, comparing/contrasting, and ending. Essentially, we use transition phrases when:

- We're **emphasizing** a point we're trying to make
- We're **expanding** on a point and offering more examples
- We're **comparing** or **contrasting** thoughts
- We're **ending** our point and summing up what was just said

The following table breaks down each category and offers some transition phrases to use when presenting.

EMPHASIZING	EXPANDING	COMPARING	CONTRASTING	ENDING
Which is why . . .	In addition . . .	Similarly . . .	On the other hand . . .	In the end . . .
The most important . . .	Plus . . .	We can also see . . .	However . . .	To sum it up . . .
Above all else . . .	On top of that . . .	Just like . . .	On the contrary . . .	In conclusion . . .
Which brings me to . . .	In fact . . .	For instance . . .	But . . .	So to bring it back . . .

Many people never think about using transition phrases when presenting, but including them can boost our audience's understanding, because we are connecting our points. Here are some examples of transition phrases in action:

- "We've seen our membership numbers grow by 35 percent month over month. We believe it's because of our renewed commitment to digital ads, **which is why** I propose increasing our advertising budget to ten thousand dollars a month." [Emphasizing]
- "We believe the most stable way to create recurring revenue streams is to have dependable assets. **For instance**, our multifamily-unit investment fund does just that." [Comparing]
- "This ADHD pill is longer-acting, lasting for sixteen hours versus the standard twelve hours. **In the end**, we would recommend our pill for those who want coverage throughout the day." [Ending]

Now let's get really tactical. We know using transition words can help with connecting our points and give the impression of ease, but when exactly do we use them? If we are presenting with a deck, it's best to use transition phrases when we're transitioning between slides. This tip is gold because chances are, when we're presenting, we're reading what's on the screen and then clicking to the next slide. That click is often done in silence, perhaps creating a pause for a second or two. It may look like this:

Get to a slide → talk about it → **pause/silence** as we
flip to the next slide → resume talking

The pause/silence, unless strategically placed, breaks the flow of our speaking. So to give the impression we are connecting the dots between our slides, we'll want to substitute a transition phrase for that silence, linking the current slide to the next. Here are some examples:

SLIDE A	**TRANSITION PHRASES** *"Which brings me to this page . . ."* *"We can also see on the next . . ."* *"So, in conclusion . . ."*	SLIDE B

Using this technique can create a beautiful flow in our speaking. It also gives the impression that we know our material.

Another tip when preparing our presentation is to nail down how we start and end. The beginning is when the strongest impressions are formed. Listeners are eager to hear us speak, so their full attention is on us. Therefore, giving our beginning a bit of TLC can ensure we are capturing our audience's attention and meeting their expectations. So, we can start off our speaking with a compelling story, startling statistics, or a reminder of our accolades to set the stage. We can also share what they can expect from our speech by saying, "My hope is at the end of my talk today, everyone will walk away knowing exactly . . ." But again, what matters most with every effective presentation is to always tailor our message to our audience.

The end of our presentation is where we'll wrap up any loose ends to create a satisfying conclusion. This ending can be a call to action, reviewing points made, or telling a great final story. It's also a place to reiterate what we said at the very beginning to create a full-circle experience. Any of these techniques can ensure we're presenting in a way that showcases our expertise while helping us build visibility at work.

COMMUNICATING WELL IS an art as well as a skill. It is also 100 percent learnable. I say this with certainty because I was fairly shy, anxious, and timid growing up, and speaking well did not come naturally. Like many people raised with Quiet Culture values, I leaned on my desire to just let my work speak for itself. However, we know that our work can only speak for itself if we are the ones pushing it forward. Everything I've covered in this chapter, including chiming in during meetings, reducing filler words, convincing people, and presenting with ease, is meant to set the groundwork so you can communicate effectively at work too. What took me years of learning and fine-tuning is now distilled into easy frameworks and sections, so you can learn and practice them. But remember, our words will have impact only if we deliver them with conviction.

Driving the Direction
of the Conversation

In the spring of 2021, the world was a little more than a year into the COVID-19 pandemic. In-person offices were shut down, and much of the corporate world was still locked in virtual or hybrid work. I was lucky enough that one of my LinkedIn Learning courses, Developing Executive Presence on Video Conference Calls, had just hit one million views, so companies were beginning to reach out and ask for virtual communications help.

It was during this period that I received a message from a large pharmaceutical company based in Canada. They wanted to help their entire sales rep team learn how to better present and sell in the virtual world.

"Our reps have always felt comfortable walking into offices and building relationships with doctors, but with virtual calls, it is much harder," said Nancy Burns, an internal senior project manager. "We need our sales reps to communicate with ease on video."

Nancy said building rapport and connection, critical in a competitive sales environment, was a challenge online. Giving presentations was also hard because there was no telling whether the other side was interested or even listening. She said it was clear that people's attention spans were shorter on video calls, and she wanted her team to elevate their communication skills.

Over the next several months, I created a custom training program for their entire sales division. I had two objectives: elevate how everyone presented on video, and help the team anticipate and address their clients' concerns with confidence.

For presenting, I homed in on teaching the reps how to reduce awkward silences, which on video can seem twice as long. I also taught them how to engage others when they toggled between folders while they shared their screen. For example, they should always explain what they were doing behind the scenes by saying things like, "I'm going to share my screen now," or "I'm going to find this folder and pull it up so you can see . . ." By explicitly looping the other person in to what they were doing, they would not leave that person wondering. We also talked about filling in any awkward moments by asking open-ended questions to keep the conversation flowing.

When anticipating and addressing concerns virtually, I also taught the reps my technique of "switching lanes." This is a speaking technique media trainers often use when they teach interviewees how to tackle tough questions without looking shocked. The Switch Lane Technique is twofold: acknowledge, then switch lanes using transitional phrases (see the following table). I trained the sales reps to hear key words that signaled concern, like, "I'm not sure" or "I'm a bit unclear." Once they heard that, the reps would acknowledge their clients by saying things like, "I hear you" and "I understand what you're saying." But the key was to not repeat the concerned word or phrase, and instead use transitional phrases to pivot. So they could say, "Well, as a matter of fact" or "And this is why we're . . ." Applying this technique gave the reps a speaking flow to communicate their expertise with confidence.

Switch Lane Technique

THEM: CONCERN	YOU: ACKNOWLEDGE	YOU: SWITCH LANES
"I'm not sure how"	"I hear what you're saying"	"In fact"
"I'm a bit unclear"	"I understand what you're saying"	"Which is why"
"I'm concerned"	"Great question"	"As a matter of fact"

WORD TO THE WISE

 When on a video call, take extra steps to ensure you set yourself up in the best light—figuratively and literally—because it can help you develop virtual executive presence. Lighting is a key feature for this because if your lighting is well-placed, others will have a better viewing experience of you. The best source of light is facing a window, because it gives your face a soft glow. Avoid having your back to a window, because that creates a dark silhouette. If you cannot adjust where you sit, adding a small desk lamp or a clip-on ring light can transform how you show up.

THE BOTTOM LINE

- Great communication is the thread that makes our Quiet Capital Framework come to life, because it helps us show up and speak up with clarity.

- In meetings, use the 4A Sequence—active listening, acknowledging, anchoring, and answering—to gauge the right time to enter a conversation, and how to do it so people listen.

- If we begin to ramble, we should ask ourselves the golden question: "What's the point I'm trying to make here?" This question will refocus our speaking.

- Marrying emotionally and quantitatively driven points is how we can create Persuasive Points, which appeal to our listeners' logic and emotion.

- The Power of the Contrast is sharing both the problem and the solution so people can get a full picture of our idea and how it can help.

- Don't rush when speaking: pause, breathe, think, and speak with conviction to control the use of filler words.

- Hedging words can soften the blow of a message.

- Feeling confident presenting involves getting into the right mindset: a presentation is a conversation, our audience only knows what we tell them, and it's an effective way to build influence and visibility.

- Using transition phrases during our presentations can connect our points and drive them home, giving the impression of ease and knowledge.

CHAPTER 8

EXPANDING OUR TONE OF VOICE

Striking the right tone

You could hear a pin drop in the classroom. Standing next to the whiteboard was our fifth-grade history teacher, Ms. Liu.

"Who was Abraham Lincoln's vice president?" she asked the class again.

That semester, we were learning about US history, and Ms. Liu posed a question to the entire classroom that no one seemed to want to answer. I had an idea what the answer might be, but there was no way I was raising my hand. I glanced down at the paper on my desk to not draw attention to myself. But from the corner of my eye, I could see Ms. Liu scanning the room looking for someone to call on. I kept my eyes down, hoping she would pass me by.

"Please don't call my name," I thought as I stared blankly at my desk.

"Jessica," she said. My body froze. "Do you know the answer?"

I looked up, startled, my eyes wide.

"Um," I said. "I am not sure, but maybe—"

"Speak louder," Ms. Liu said.

"Um, Andrew Johnson?" I responded.

"Your voice is too soft. We can't hear you. Please speak up!"

"Andrew Johnson," I repeated louder. I could feel my face getting bright red.

"That's right."

For many years, my "soft voice" was a frequent topic of discussion. Teachers, aunts, and uncles would often say I was too soft-spoken, and it was hard for them to hear me. This wasn't entirely a surprise because I knew where my soft voice came from. It was my gut reaction to when people would look at me and I wanted to redirect their gaze.

To be clear, just because we come from a Quiet Culture, it doesn't mean we all are naturally soft-spoken. Many of us speak just fine and people can hear us well, but the uncomfortable *feeling* of being put on the spot is the same. When we are the center of attention, many of us find our speaking changes. We talk fast or softly, or we end our sentences in an upward tone, just to punt the conversation off to someone else. In my case, I didn't like the spotlight, and I certainly didn't think much about adjusting my tone. In my mind, I figured that if I could write the correct answer on paper and do the work well, that was all that mattered.

Fast-forward ten years later and I was now an intern in a Loud Culture newsroom. Everything I knew about tone was turned upside down when I heard my colleagues speak on-air.

In the office, the environment was as you'd expect it: loud— TVs blaring, people shouting across the room, the constant clicking of keyboard keys, and the never-ending ringing of calls coming into the station. But when the clock hit the top of the news hour, everything in the room screeched to a halt because the hourly newscast would begin. Instead of the commotion, the deep, commanding voices of the anchors and reporters would radiate through the room. As a young intern immersing myself in this environment, I was captivated by the richness and variety of tone used by the anchors and reporters. They all talked with an intentionality that created resonance.

For months, I tried to decipher what it was about their voices that made them so easy to listen to. How were they so clear, and how did they alter their voices so fluidly that every word had the right pitch, inflection, and tonality? After a few months of interning at the TV station, the answer to how they did it started to crystallize. Each person's speaking voice was deliberate. Each word had purpose, and every dip, lift, or pause had intent. As a person coming from a Quiet Culture, I found this intentionality in speaking striking. I had never realized there was such a musical element to voice, and the way those on TV used this element was fascinating. It wasn't about their speaking loudly or a lot, it was *how* they used their voices that mattered. It was as if each person could alter the energy of the room by just controlling the tone of their voice.

In the previous chapter, we discussed how certain words can maximize our speaking impact. In this chapter, we will talk about the second pillar of impactful speaking: tone. Some of the most influential communicators have a speaking tone that is undeniably dynamic. We know it when we hear it, because their tone is easy to listen to, clear, and commanding. An influential speaker may not say much, but when they do talk, others listen.

To be the kind of communicator others want to listen to, we have to learn the fundamentals of tone, because it can either compel people to stay engaged or make them disengage. Think about it this way: when we listen to music, sometimes we skip a song because the musical notes or pitch don't call to us. Or more pointedly, we tune out people's talking when they speak in a monotone voice for an extended period of time. As humans, we tune out sounds we don't like, consciously and unconsciously. However, in the working world, when we speak, our intention is for others to listen. This includes when we present to a group, talk about our work, or even ask for what we want. We want people to pay attention. So how can we maximize our chances of this happening? According to Dr. Wendy LeBorgne, a voice pathologist, communications consultant, and TEDx speaker, there are five tonal elements that make up the sound of our voice.

1. **Frequency:** The pitch of one's voice, which can be either high or low. Men typically have lower pitches and women higher pitches.
2. **Rate:** The pace of our speaking. When people get nervous, they tend to speak fast. But when someone speaks too slowly, they can seem unenthused.

3. **Intensity:** The volume of our voice. A loud voice can be perceived as aggressive or yelling. But if a voice is too soft, it can signal shyness or low energy.

4. **Inflection:** The fluid upward and downward trend of our voice. Those with a consistent downward inflection can sound monotone, and those with an upward inflection can sound unsure.

5. **Quality:** The innate sound of our voice, whether it is raspy, hoarse, nasal, and so on. It is unique to us and is how people know it's us when we answer the phone. Each person's vocal quality is different.

Of the five elements, the last one, quality, is the only one we cannot change. If you think about it, who are some of the most recognizable actors and actresses out there? You know them because of the quality of their voice. For example, Morgan Freeman's voice is iconic because of its deep timbre. Meryl Streep's voice has a resonant quality to it, because her intonations can be soft. And Awkwafina, aka Nora Lum, has a lower-pitched, raspy voice. All three are distinctive and unique. According to LeBorgne, this distinctiveness is what makes us distinguishable.

When thinking about how we can use our tone of voice at work to draw people in when we speak, we need to focus on the four modifiable elements: frequency, rate, intensity, and inflection.

FREQUENCY

Think back to the last time you listened to a great audiobook. Were you totally immersed and captivated? How much of it was the narrator's tone that got you hooked? Chances are, you probably didn't even think about it, because you were so entranced by the story. For the listener, this is a good thing, because any vocal peculiarities can detract from the content itself. However, for a narrator, speaking into a microphone is a careful and deliberate process. If they want to build anticipation for a scene, they may raise their pitch a bit higher to create a state of tension. Or if they want to convey passion and emotion, they may gently raise and then lower their voice to create depth and ambiance. Whatever scene it is, they are guiding their audience by adjusting the pitch of their voice.

In the professional world, while we know men generally have a lower pitch and women have a higher pitch, we all have a pitch range. Being an effective communicator means using this range with purpose, just like the narrators we listen to. A good rule of thumb is to speak at a higher pitch when showing enthusiasm; but if we want to convey authority and seriousness, we should speak at a lower pitch. What is also worth noting when talking about pitch is having *resonance*. A pitch that has resonance also has depth, and we all know it when we hear it. It's a rich tone both men and women can achieve.

To find your resonance, you'll want to ensure you are relaxed, because tension can hinder it. Start by humming. The sound of your hum is your baseline pitch. From there, hum higher and hum lower. Get comfortable doing it at a range so it sounds melodic. Keep humming until you get those nerves out. (Yes, you will feel silly doing it, but it's OK! You have to get over that funny feeling to hum authentically, just like if you were humming in the shower.) Now, with that hum range, did you feel a vibration in the back of your throat? Did you also get a sense that the sound was coming from the pit of your stomach? If not, try again. That feeling—the vibration in your throat, the sound coming from deep within—is what you're trying to achieve when you speak, so you have that depth. A resonant voice comes from your diaphragm.

You may discover as you're speaking from that deeper place that you feel out of breath. To overcome that, you have to be intentional with your breathing. The best communicators know how to marry breathing and speaking, similar to how runners synchronize their pace with their breath.

"Posture and breathing are everything," one veteran reporter told me early in my career. "You have to tell yourself to project your voice so it's coming from a deeper place—the pit of your stomach."

The bottom line: "The only way you're going to get better is to practice out loud," he said.

Here's a guide to combining breathing with diaphragmatic speaking:

1. Take two or three deep breaths. The key is to relax your body. Your chest and lungs will expand as you

breathe in to allow more air into your respiratory system. Notice how it feels.

2. Once relaxed, notice your posture: straighten your spine, lift your chin, and roll your shoulders back. These changes in posture will help you project.

3. Now, breathe in and out again and speak from the lower part of your stomach. Remember your humming range? It should feel as if your words are being pushed from your stomach instead of your throat. Imagine projecting your voice so a person at the other end of the room can hear you.

If you need to, take this book and try reading certain sections out loud. It *will* feel awkward, but push forward. Reading out loud is the best way for you to play around with your pitch and find what feels natural to you.

Eric Chen is the founder of Sabobatage: The Boba Card Game, the first Asian-inspired boba card game in the US. He is also my younger brother, whom we met in previous chapters. Eric was first introduced to the concept of marrying breath with his speaking when he started working as a sales associate at the payroll software company ADP. As a young college grad, he realized he needed to develop his executive presence when speaking with clients so he could convince and persuade them.

"One of the first things my mentor told me was I needed to work on my communication skills, specifically my speaking presence," Eric recalled.

Coming from a Quiet Culture, he never thought too much about the sound of his voice. Like many of us, he was of the mentality that speaking loudly (to be heard) was all that mattered with his tone. But now that he was forced to speak and sell to strangers, building his credibility and authority was critical. He had to learn how to speak with tonality, master his elevator pitch, and deliver words with intent.

"I wanted to get better so I could close more deals. This mentor was serious about me taking the time to improve my speaking voice."

Eric said one of the first things he did was find an affordable and convenient way to practice. That ended up being using his phone to record himself speaking and then listening to it to find areas of improvement.

"I remember I committed to doing this at least once a week for one hour. I even asked to record some of my client calls just to hear myself," Eric said. "One of the things I noticed was I talked in a higher pitch and faster when I would get nervous. But there was no way I would've known it if I didn't listen to myself."

He was right—frequency is very much linked to speed, which goes into the second point of our tone of voice: our rate.

RATE

It was a bright and sunny morning in San Diego, and I was heading in to work ready to meet with our TV consultant.

Every few years, TV stations around the country hire consultants to evaluate and give feedback to those who work on-air. They critique numerous elements of our presentation, including our clothes, hair, and makeup, and how we carry ourselves when we speak. While it can be brutally humbling, it's also necessary to get this external feedback so we know how to better communicate in public.

As I sat down in our large conference room with the consultant by my side, she pulled out her laptop, and opened the screen to a video of me.

"Let's watch this news story you did last week," she said.

As the video played, I saw myself pointing and gesturing as I spoke. "Not bad," I thought. There was fluidity in my speaking, and I sounded clear and concise. I also accentuated my thoughts with deliberate body language to drive my point home. The consultant paused the video.

"I like how you used your hands to demonstrate what you're saying," she said, "but you really need to speak slower."

Baffled by her feedback, I said, "I thought I was already speaking slowly."

"You have to speak very slowly, much slower than you think," she replied. "This gives the perception of gravitas."

If tone of voice was something I never considered growing up in a Quiet Culture, then gravitas was a concept from Mars. While I knew what this word meant, the act of exhibiting it had never entered my mind until this very moment. In a nutshell, gravitas is having weight or heaviness in our speaking, and it creates an aura of seriousness, dignity, and importance. In a

Quiet Culture, gravitas is typically associated with age and experience, similar to credibility. However, in a Loud Culture, age or title is just a small contributing factor to having gravitas at work. Anyone, just by their speaking, can exude that authority and composure too. But how? By speaking slowly. When we speak fast, we appear rushed and frantic—not great for developing gravitas. Instead, we need to slow down to create the impression we're calm and collected. The good news is that rate is one of the easier elements to adjust, because we likely have an inkling of when we're speaking too fast. When this happens, we have to acknowledge it, remind ourselves to adjust it, and then slow down. While it's easier said than done, a simple way to remember this is to take a sticky note, write "slow down," and tape it near your computer. It's not fancy, but it is an effective way to remind ourselves to slow down when we're about to jump into a meeting.

With that being said, another way to level up our speaking rate and build gravitas is to sometimes speak faster. (Yes, speaking faster has its value too!) However, there's a key difference: it's all about intention. Varying our speed is how we can draw our audience in, because it keeps things interesting. But how do we know when to speed up and when to slow down? We should speed up slightly when we're explaining or giving examples, and slow down when we're homing in on our conclusion or takeaway. Slowing down gives others time to absorb and process what we've just said. Remember the golden question: *What's the point I'm trying to make here?* The answer should always be delivered slowly.

Take a look at the following sentences and practice saying them out loud. Slow down when reading the bold sections; otherwise, speak at your normal pace.

- "We've seen our membership numbers grow by **35 percent month over month**. We believe it's because of our renewed commitment to digital ads, which is why I propose we increase our advertising budget to **ten thousand dollars a month**."

- "The most stable way to create **recurring revenue streams** is to have **dependable assets**. For instance, our **multifamily-unit investment fund** does just that, and we'd love to send over some materials to you."

- "This ADHD pill is **longer acting**, lasting for **sixteen hours versus the standard twelve hours**. In the end, we would recommend our pill for those who want coverage **throughout the day**."

As you continue to hone your rate, you will soon be able to identify when to slow down and when to speed up. Next, let's talk about intensity.

The Marriage of Tone, Speed, and Flow

One of my clients, James Acosta, was preparing for his company's Series C fundraising round. While already running a successful company worth hundreds of millions of dollars, James wanted to level up his presentation skills. So on a Thursday morning, we jumped into our weekly video meeting and James began presenting. Within seconds, he launched into the details of his company, talking about numbers and speaking a mile a minute.

The numbers were dense. The speed at which he was running through them was hard to follow. I was overwhelmed and feeling utterly disconnected from his message.

"Let's pause for a second," I interrupted.

Having worked with James for several weeks now, I knew one of the most compelling aspects of his company was its competitive advantage. "Don't bury the lede," I told him. "Start with that, not all those numbers you just brain-dumped at once."

I reminded him that when presenting, flow of content mattered. So instead of jumping straight into the numbers and statistics, he needed to capture his listeners' attention. I unveiled my favorite presentation format for him to follow:

1. Start by thanking everyone for taking the time to join the meeting by using words like *thrilled*, *excited*, *looking forward*.

2. Briefly introduce the presentation topic.
3. Share two or three main takeaways that the audience will get out of the presentation.
4. Say one sentence encompassing the feeling you'd like everyone to have; for example: *My hope is at the end of this presentation, everyone here will walk away with a clearer understanding / a solid framework / a good idea of . . .*
5. Then introduce yourself and explain why you're credible to discuss this topic.

As James reconfigured his deck to match this flow, I reminded him he needed to control his speed too.

After his second attempt, I asked him how the process of speaking felt.

"Having this clear flow makes speaking feel more natural. I also feel like I am giving myself more time to think about what I want to say and how I want to deliver it," he replied.

James said he began thinking of his rate as a game. He would identify the appropriate time to adjust his rate and change his speed accordingly—much like a NASCAR driver navigating curves and straightaways. He was now anticipating the turns and driving on the offense, not defense.

WORD TO THE WISE

 The same script can sound entirely different when two people read it. That's because different people emphasize different words and phrases. And that is the thing—our tone of voice can be both an art and a style. It's important to spend time practicing finding your speaking voice. Recording yourself reading out loud is one of the most effective ways to identify when and how you can make adjustments. In fact, the most impactful speakers know delivery is sometimes more important to perfect than the content itself.

INTENSITY

For years, I attributed the sound of one's voice only to intensity—essentially, how loud or soft we speak. When we tell our partner, "Hey, watch your tone!" we're likely referring to intensity. However, we know volume is only one fifth of the equation.

When it comes to our speaking intensity, we often leave it to chance because it's how we *feel* in that moment. For example, when we're excited or angry, we speak louder. When we're uncomfortable or anxious, we speak softer. Or if we're not feeling any sort of way, we stay neutral. However, to really leverage our intensity so it's smart, not loud, we have to use it with intention. For instance, if we want our team to lean in to the severity or urgency of our message, we should strategically soften our tone. Or if we want our manager to get excited about our idea, we should speak a bit louder so they can sense our excitement. Our intensity—loud or soft—is how we can draw people in the way we want. It can influence how our message is received and perceived.

If the way we control our intensity sounds like how we manage our speaking rate, you're right. We can combine both elements so they harmonize. The most impactful speakers mix both, because it makes their speaking interesting and compelling. Here's a breakdown of what this looks like:

INTENTION	INTENSITY AND RATE ELEMENTS
Joyful messaging	loud intensity, fast rate
Serious messaging	medium intensity, slow rate
Sad messaging	soft intensity, slow rate
Matter-of-fact	medium intensity, medium rate
Powerful	medium intensity, slow rate

When we marry our intensity and our rate, we have the ability to pull people in the way we want to. Because if we think about the moments we speak, whether it's to convince others of our idea, advocate for ourselves, or even say no (all concepts we talked about in part 2), we have influence over how our audience thinks of us, as long as we control *how* we speak. Next, let's look at inflection.

INFLECTION

For more than thirteen years, my Saturday mornings were dedicated to attending weekend Mandarin school. This was a nonnegotiable learning experience, because my parents wanted to ensure I retained this part of my Chinese heritage while living in the US.

"Jessica, one day you will appreciate learning Mandarin," my parents would often say.

While these classes were torturous because I certainly preferred to sleep on weekend mornings, alas, my parents were right. Being able to speak and understand a second language is an asset; it has opened doors personally and professionally. Today, my ability to speak Mandarin has given me a presence in Asia through my company, Soulcast Media. But it was during weekend Chinese school that I learned the formalities of the language, such as how every word had an associated inflection (i.e., intonation), which, if used incorrectly, could change the word entirely. In Mandarin, there are five to consider:

| Flat | Up | Down and Up | Down | Neutral |

Unlike in Mandarin, inflections in English aren't as precise. A change in inflection at the end of a word or sentence doesn't change its meaning, but it does change its impact. When it comes to using our tone effectively, matching our inflection with our intent is important. If we are trying to convey certainty, we should say the last few words with a downward inflection. This gives the impression we mean what we say. For example:

- I believe option B is a better idea (downward inflection).
- I'm concerned the way we're addressing the client's issues is causing more confusion (downward inflection).

On the flip side, if we end our sentence with an upward inflection, so that it sounds like a question, it gives the impression we're unsure. Just take those two sentences earlier and put an upward inflection on the last few words. Doesn't the sentence feel less impactful? In the communication world, we call the upward inflection "uptalk" or "upspeak." In recent decades, there has been a trend toward increased uptalk in our speaking. This isn't a problem if we're actually asking a question, but if we're not, an upward inflection can make our statement seem less assertive.

It is important to note when uptalk has its value. We can use uptalk if we are trying to convey uncertainty. We can also use it to hedge how we insert ourselves into conversations, such as when we say, "Excuse me." Ending that phrase with an upward inflection generally sounds less forceful and abrasive. But again, we use uptalk because we intended to.

WE JUST COVERED the four elements of tone that we can actively control. However, I would be remiss if I did not mention enunciation when talking about voice. While enunciation isn't part of the five elements of tone, how we enunciate our words has a significant impact on the perception of our speaking. The opposite of enunciating is mumbling. To overcome mumbling, we need to hone one of my favorite speaking techniques: focusing on the first and last few letters of a word. It's simple and effective, particularly for those who don't speak English as their first language.

Here are some words for you to practice out loud. Be mindful of emphasizing the beginning and end for clarity:

POWER	STRONG
CONFIDENCE	INCONSEQUENTIAL
IMPROVEMENT	THUNDER
SPEAKING	IMMUNOTHERAPY
AUTHENTIC	RESEARCH

Now, practice the following sentences out loud and make sure you're enunciating both the first and last letters of each word, while also being mindful of your rate (bolded words indicate where to slow down):

- Once we become a strategic communicator, we will no longer **leave our delivery to chance**. For example, we can walk into a presentation and know how to speak in a way that has variety. Or if we walk into a meeting with senior managers, we'll be able to **instinctively adjust our voice** so others can hear our assurance.

In my work with non-native English speakers, many of whom were raised in a Quiet Culture, I have found that the innate desire to stay out of the spotlight can cause words to sound muffled. Whether it's because they feel self-conscious about their accent or they overanalyze the situation, their muffled words can hinder the impact of their delivery. I have discovered the most common words that get muffled have "in" or "th" in them. When it's said, "in" sounds like "im," and "th" has a "f" sound. For example, *injustice* will sound like "imjustice," and *something* will sound like "somefing." Enunciating these words carefully can make a difference in how clear you sound. If you're unsure whether this is something that affects you, simply record yourself speaking, and you'll be able to hear this instantly. Even if you are a native English speaker, practicing your enunciation can enhance your speaking clarity.

Thinking back to those early months when I was soaking up the sights and sounds of a Loud Culture newsroom, I realize now that tone was a critical element for building speaking presence. It was also a great tool for someone with a Quiet Culture background to develop more speaking authority, because I didn't have to be loud or aggressive to be noticed. Instead, I just needed to speak with intention and toggle between different frequencies, rates, intensities, and inflections. As long as I focused on tone, I could control my message and ensure it landed the way I wanted it to. An influential speaker doesn't have to say much; they just need to know *how* to say it so others will listen.

THE BOTTOM LINE

- Our tone of voice can be broken down into five elements: frequency, rate, intensity, inflection, and quality.

- The quality of our voice can't be changed, because it's unique to us.

- Speaking from the diaphragm, or using our "stomach voice," can create depth and speaking presence, which is linked to frequency.

- Varying our rate of speaking between fast and slow can accentuate the point we're trying to make.

- Mixing our intensity between loud and soft can draw listeners in, because variety keeps our speaking interesting.

- Inflection and intention go hand in hand.

- Enunciating prevents mumbling. Focusing on the first and last letters of a word can clarify our speaking.

CHAPTER 9

UTILIZING OUR BODY LANGUAGE

What others see when we speak

My heart was racing, and I could hear the countdown loud in my ears.

"We are going live in three, two, one . . ."

I took a deep breath and whispered, "It's showtime!"

Staring straight into the camera lens, I began speaking, tilting my head ever so slightly left and right as the words rolled through the teleprompter screen. Periodically, my eyebrows would rise to build warmth when reading a heartwarming story, and then furrow gently to show concern when talking about a serious issue. My hands lifted as I emphasized certain words, and I laid them back down once I was done. My chest was wide, and my shoulders were down. I summoned all the nonverbal cues I knew to complement the words I was saying to display confidence and ease.

"You did great!" my manager said as I walked off the studio set. "You looked comfortable in the anchor chair."

I beamed with pride. It was exactly what I wanted to hear. All the months I had spent advocating for myself to get to the anchor chair finally paid off. Now I had to prove that I could actually do it. Because the truth was, I was not confident. I was a ball of nervous energy inside. My heart was racing, and my hands were sweaty. While reading through the lines in the teleprompter, I couldn't help but pray I wouldn't stumble over a word or fumble through a story. Because in my mind, this was the one shot that could make or break future opportunities. Fortunately, from what my manager could see, nothing in my body language signaled that I was nervous or anxious. And for that, I was thankful.

But to even get to this point where I could give the impression of speaking with ease and confidence while feeling totally nervous inside was a long and winding journey. Coming from a Quiet Culture, I never learned or even thought about the art of communicating, particularly nonverbal communication skills, until I started working.

I grew up in a home where, frankly, my parents rarely showed emotion or physical displays of affection. Body language as a means of expressing oneself was limited. The only time I ever saw intentional body language was on TV. For example, I remember thinking how unusual it was for family members to hug each other so affectionately when they were happy and for them to use so many hand gestures when speaking. Or even the explicitness of saying "I love you" felt foreign, as if someone were speaking another language. This didn't mean I felt a lack of love or affection while being raised in a Quiet Culture; showing emotion verbally and nonverbally was just done in other, quieter ways. For example, sentiments of "I care about you" and "I am thinking of you" were translated to "Make sure you eat enough" and "Stay warm when you're outside." However, when I entered a Loud Culture workplace and saw the overt displays of emotion, even from strangers, my Quiet Culture upbringing had me thinking: *Wow, people are pretty expressive in this loud working world.*

As different as it was, I didn't stay stuck deciphering the differences for too long; being immersed in a Loud Culture newsroom, I had to learn how to express my ideas clearly and confidently, and to do it in a way that felt right. Fortunately, I didn't have to look far. In the TV world, all intonations and gestures are dissected, measured, and observed to ensure they match our message. To say working on TV was like getting a front-row seat in learning communication skills would have been an understatement. One of the first things I uncovered was that our communication is made up of our words, our tone of voice, and our body language. Of the three, our body language makes the biggest impact on our speaking abilities. It accounts for 55 percent of the impression people have of us; our tone of voice is 38 percent, and our actual words are only 7 percent.

For those of us raised in a Quiet Culture, if direct and explicit communication is not our style, nonverbal communication can be music to our ears, because it's a tool that can allow us to convey our message without saying much at all; we can use what we do with our body to magnify the point we're trying to make. For a subset of us, this might be something we're already doing without even realizing it. As keen observers, we are taking in our environment and its people, and we are picking up nonverbal cues quickly. A slight move of a person's eyes, or the way they gesture with their arms—we notice it all. But as good as we are at being perceptive of others, we can let our own nonverbal cues fall to the wayside, unless we think about them proactively. The following section is meant to distill years of nonverbal communication practice into a few key sections, so you can learn exactly what to do and how to do it, to give yourself a communication advantage.

THE NONVERBAL FOUR

To communicate intentionally with our body language, we first have to see what we're working with. Let's look at body language in four quadrants from the top down: our head/facial expressions, shoulders/chest, arms/hands, and legs/feet. I call these the nonverbal four. Each of these areas, when used strategically, can signal a particular positive or negative expression. This chart is a good rule of thumb to follow.

BODY	POSITIVE	SIGNALS	NEGATIVE	SIGNALS
Head/Facial Expressions	Tilted toward the speaker or audience; looking down momentarily while nodding head when thinking	Focus or understanding	Eyes darting around the room	Indifference or uncertainty
Shoulders/ Chest	Shoulders rolled back, squared toward the action; leaning in but chest still wide	Engaged	Shoulders high and stiff near ears; slouching with chest caved in	Anxious or bored
Arms/ Hands	*When observing:* To the side or on the table to take up space *When speaking:* Slow gestures to accentuate points, holding up relevant items	Comfortable and confident	Hands in pocket or tucked into crossed arms, quick movements	Nervous or noncommittal
Legs/Feet	*When sitting:* Legs crossed or in a figure-four with an ankle over the opposite knee *When standing:* Feet about 12–18 inches apart	Alert	Tapping one's toes, fidgety	Uncertain, uncomfortable, or nervous

When you look at this table, know that every movement sends a message, whether it's intentional or not. So, treat this as a guide to what your body language is signaling. Now, let's get into the details of each of the nonverbal four so we can maximize our speaking impact.

Head Movement and Facial Expressions

When we meet someone for the first time, our brain is working in high gear. We are listening, evaluating, and making a conscious or subconscious decision about whether we trust that person or not. Similar to creating our elevator pitch, building credibility with new people happens quickly. Neuroscientists at Harvard University and New York University say two parts of our brain light up when we form an impression of someone: our amygdala, which is linked to emotional learning, and our posterior cingulate cortex, which is linked to decision-making. Both are furiously processing what we're seeing in real time and creating an impression of the person we're speaking with.

"Even when we only briefly encounter others, brain regions that are important in forming evaluations are engaged, resulting in a quick first impression," said Elizabeth Phelps of NYU, where the study was conducted.

Forming these impressions happens fast; it takes literally seconds—specifically, seven seconds. Now, if we flip the script, when someone meets us for the first time, they are likely going through the same process in their head. They want to know whether they can trust us too. With so much riding on just a few seconds, how can we come off the way we want? This is where we will talk about our facial expressions. The way we move our head when speaking, the way we smile, and even where we look are all nonverbal cues that can signal how we feel, including how comfortable and confident we are in that moment.

Let's begin with our eyes. For those of us raised in a Quiet Culture, eye contact can be tricky because, depending on who we're with, looking people in the eye can feel unnatural, especially when there is a perceived power distance. In some cultures, eye contact can even be perceived as disrespectful. However, when working in a Loud Culture, maintaining eye contact, especially when we are trying to drive a point home, is how we can show others we are confident and assured in what we're saying. In fact, research has shown that people find it attractive when the person they're speaking with makes eye contact with them, as avoiding it may signal they're nervous or uncertain. While it's easy to maintain eye contact when we're comfortable, what do we do when we're stumped or put on the spot?

One of my most popular trainings is teaching people how to handle tough situations while maintaining their executive presence. The technique I teach is called the Down-Up-Point Movement; it is a way of staying composed when we are unsure of what to say. To begin, draw your eyes **down**, and slightly nod your head to acknowledge the question. This gives the impression that you're thinking even though you may not know the answer. After a few seconds, look **up**, make eye contact with the person you're talking to, and state your **pointed** response. This movement is powerful because when you are stumped, you may instinctively start to look away, or your eyes may widen and your brows jolt up. These movements signal we have been thrown off guard or we're in shock.

As for the pointed response, your answer can be as simple as: "Great question, let me get back to you," or "I don't have the answers to your question now, but I will follow up." Responding in this matter-of-fact way, while maintaining eye contact, is how we can show we're in control and minimize our use of filler words.

In chapter 7, we shared tips on presenting with ease, including getting into the right mindset, connecting our points, and focusing on transition words. While these are critical to creating a nice speaking flow, where we look can be a telltale sign of whether we feel comfortable when public speaking or not. For those of us raised in a Quiet Culture, getting up in front of an audience can ignite our deepest fears. So if you cannot bear to look at your audience because it reminds you that you're being watched, a good alternative is to look at the tops of people's heads. To do this, glide your eyes around the room scanning people's heads, because at minimum, you are looking in the right direction, not letting your eyes dart all over the place or staring at the floor or ceiling.

Similarly, Jerry Kang, distinguished professor of law at UCLA, gives this advice when counseling nervous students how to present confidently: "If you're talking to groups, try to make it so it's to one particular listener, at least at one moment in the conversation." He said he'll first scan the room, find a person to make eye contact with, lock it in for a few seconds, complete the point, and then move on to the next person. "It'll feel like he or she is the only person in the room, and I'm only talking to them," said Kang.

While our eyes can speak volumes, our smile is what can get people to really lean in to what we're saying. Research has shown people who have happier faces are seen as more trustworthy. If we combine smiling with raising our eyebrows, also known as the eyebrow flash, we can increase our likability when engaging with others. But it is important to note, there is a difference between a genuine smile and a social smile. Many of us may not think of our smile in this way, but we know the difference when we see it. In social smiling, our lips form the shape of a smile, but nothing else on our face shows we're happy. But a genuine smile, on the other hand, is when our cheeks rise and our eyes narrow. Look at these two images and notice the difference in how you feel. Which person would you gravitate toward?

SMILES

Social Smile   Genuine Smile

So remember, if we're speaking to convince, persuade, or pitch, genuinely smiling is a powerful way to communicate. It's also great for building credibility, because smiling while talking can build trust. Combine that with strategic eye movement, and our communication skills can feel a lot more powerful.

Our Hands Are an Asset

In 2015, I started my third job as a news reporter—this time at ABC in San Diego. Having already worked at NBC in Reno and at Time Warner Cable News in the greater New York City area, I thought I had a good understanding of how to deliver a compelling news story. But from week one, I saw there was a lot more to learn. My manager at this new station had a very specific idea of what made for engaging communication, and it centered around what we did with our hands when speaking.

"Never have your hands glued to your side when you speak," she would say. "You need to draw others in by *showing* them what you're talking about." To her, our job as reporters was to ensure we captured and maintained our audience's attention so viewers didn't switch channels. Using our hands, in her mind, was a visual asset. So she advised us to find something to hold or gesture to in order to drive our point home. For example, if we were talking about a book, we held that book. Or if we were talking about a tree, we pointed to a tree in the distance. Or if we had nothing to show, we used our hands to emphasize the point we were making, by, for example, moving them apart to signal something big, or lifting them up to chest level to make a point. The key was to avoid standing stiff as a board when speaking.

In 2015, Bill Gates gave what is now one of the most popular TED Talks on the platform. Titled "The Next Outbreak? We're Not Ready," it was a harbinger of what was to come just five years later when the coronavirus pandemic hit the world. That talk has since garnered over forty-five million views.

But it wasn't just the topic that made the speech resonate (and go viral), it was also how Gates presented the information. Before he even said a word, he walked onto the stage pushing a large, military-grade barrel on a hand truck. He parked it, walked to center stage, and began speaking.

"When I was a kid, the disaster we worried about most was a nuclear war. That's why we had a barrel like this down in our basement, filled with cans of food and water," Gates said, gesturing toward the barrel.

"When the nuclear attack came, we were supposed to go downstairs, hunker down, and eat out of that barrel.

"Today the greatest risk of global catastrophe doesn't look like this," he continued, referring to an image of a mushroom cloud on the screen behind him. He then pointed to a photo of a virus on the screen. "Instead, it looks like this."

In less than two minutes, Gates had his audience hooked with his demonstrative movements, which married motion and words. Now, realistically, most of us aren't going to use such a dramatic prop when speaking in our team meetings. But what we can take away is the fact that Gates didn't just stand there with his hands glued to his sides when speaking. He was gesturing and emphasizing his words with his hands, guiding the audience where to look in the process. We can easily apply these same techniques when speaking at work, including when giving presentations. In fact, finding ways to use our hands can elevate how we are perceived because it can bolster how well listeners comprehend our message.

So what are some tactical hand movements you can use when speaking? Here's a short list to get you started. What's important is to match your movement with your intention.

INTENTION	MOVEMENT
Driving a point home	Push both hands forward
Building trust	Show open palms
Showing hope	Cross two fingers together
Displaying quantity	Hold up specific number of fingers
Conveying disapproval	Clench fists

Remember, it's all about being intentional; our gestures should complement our words and reinforce our message. While our hands can be an asset when used strategically, there's also a flip side: letting them roam unchecked can be very distracting, or even upsetting. If there is no purpose to our hand movements, the intended impact can fall flat. Consider these potential (unintentional) impacts:

- Making erratic hand movements can make us appear frantic and ill at ease.
- Pointing at people can make them feel threatened.
- Crossing our arms can make us appear defensive.
- Scratching ourselves can indicate nerves and uncertainty.
- Keeping our hands frozen by our sides can make us appear stiff and uncomfortable.
- Stuffing our hands in our pockets can indicate shyness.

If we're about to jump into a video meeting, it's important to remember that communication is still very much a visual experience. What we do with our hands (or not) can signal how we're feeling. An easy way to implement intentional hand movements, especially when we're giving a virtual presentation, is to take our hands off our mouse or keyboard and use them to enhance the point we're making.

Shoulders and Posture

Our parents were right: good posture is indeed important. All those taps to tell us to straighten up so we weren't slouching were for good reason, and in the communications world, there's a practicality to it as well. Our shoulders and posture convey an unspoken message about how we're feeling, especially when we're speaking. Good posture conveys an air of confidence and certainty, while bad posture can indicate a lack of self-assurance and even insecurity.

Lung-Nien Lee, chairman of Citi Private Bank, South Asia, said that despite reaching one of the top positions at his global organization and being well respected, he still thinks about his posture when meeting with his team and stakeholders. He said he's even made a game out of reminding himself to straighten up before entering a meeting.

"When I walk through doorways, I imagine there's an apple hanging down from the doorframe. Then, I'll take a bite [in my mind]," said Lee. "Let me tell you, it straightens you up."

According to a study by Coastal Carolina University, researchers found a correlation between posture and how we feel about ourselves. Those who have a straighter posture—sitting or standing upright—tend to rate themselves as having more leadership abilities. They also reported feeling more confident, so they acted more powerfully, such as by choosing to sit closer to the head of the table instead of in the back.

Angela Jia Kim is the founder of Savor Beauty, a natural skin-care brand inspired by Korean beauty rituals. While training as a classical pianist and touring the United States and Europe as a soloist, she carefully studied the link between presence and posture. "I think [posture] was one of the most important skills I learned as a pianist," said Kim.

"Somebody who has total control over their body will command a lot more presence than somebody who is looser. I make sure the way I'm walking, my posture, everything is very elegant, poised, and commanding."

When walking into your next meeting, how can you think about your posture so it sends the right signal? First, let's think about our spine. Is it straight? If we're hunched over, it can indicate a lack of enthusiasm and energy. For shoulders, if we keep them down and relaxed, it shows we're comfortable and we're ready to engage. Let's also look at whether our chest is wide or caved in. Widening can show our readiness and that we're present.

But what do we do when we're in a virtual meeting, meaning, when we don't have to walk into a room and think about our posture? In my most popular LinkedIn Learning course, Developing Executive Presence on Video Conference Calls, I talk about how posture matters virtually as well. The video "Positioning Your Camera" is one of my favorites, because I paint the dramatic before-and-after effects of how our posture looks just by how we position our camera. For example, to show we are present and feeling confident, we need others to see our posture. So, we need to sit two to three feet away from the camera lens and tilt the camera so it is at eye level. We don't want to be too close or have the camera angle coming from below, because it will make us look like a floating head. Or if our camera is positioned too high, the focus will be on our forehead, which is not the most flattering. Making these small adjustments can transform how we show up and how we are perceived.

IN THE END, body language can make our communication more engaging and impactful if we use it to our advantage. For those of us raised with Quiet Culture values, noticing other people's nonverbal cues might come naturally. But what's equally important is for us to think about what we're doing with our body language. When we marry our body language with what we're saying, we can magnify the point we're making so it sticks. The more deliberate we are, the better the chances we have in getting noticed exactly the way we want to be.

Body Language Is like a Fine Wine Paired with a Delicious Dish

Alan Abrams is a renowned expert in the fintech industry. Recently, he was promoted to a high-profile position at his company and found himself needing to polish his public-speaking skills. His new role required him to take on more public-facing activities, including being interviewed on TV to talk about the company and their product. For Alan, this new aspect of his job was both exciting and challenging, because it was different from the behind-the-scenes work he was used to. But because he was doing a lot more of it, he knew he had to get better at it, and quickly.

As Alan and I jumped on our first call, I pulled up a video of him and his latest TV interview. Within the first few seconds, I could see he was giving all the cues that signaled he was uncomfortable and anxious. His eyes darted from the interviewer straight to the table. His posture was hunched over. And his hands were nowhere to be seen.

To help him improve, we started by pulling up a video of an executive he wanted to emulate. This CEO was being interviewed on CNBC, and his body language was giving all the cues that he was comfortable and even enjoying himself. His hand gestures were deliberate and had a fluidity that helped accentuate his points. His shoulders were squared toward the interviewer, which showed he was present and listening. And after each question, the CEO smiled and nodded thoughtfully before giving his response. His ease was palpable.

Alan and I talked about that interview, and over the next few weeks, we practiced replicating it. We worked on him slowly nodding his head as he listened to the questions being asked, which signaled he was thinking and processing. We also worked on him leaving his hands on the table so they would be easier to pull up when emphasizing a point. We ensured he gave facial cues, such as flashing a genuine smile at the beginning of the interview and maintaining eye contact when speaking. To make sure he saw how he was progressing, we conducted mock interviews and recorded them. We replayed them and practiced over and over again until these gestures began to feel like they were part of his natural communication style.

Here's a breakdown of a mock Q&A practice:

JESSICA: *Alan, what's the company hoping to achieve over the next five years?*

ALAN: Great question [*pause and smile*]. We have big plans [*open palms*] for the company [*lower hands*]. In fact, we're just scratching the surface here [*graze the top of the table*]. In the next year [*use one hand and push out*], we hope to enter the market in both APAC [*gesture left*] and EMEA [*gesture right*].

Incorporating intentional body movement into our speaking takes practice, but if we do it right, it is like pairing a perfect wine with our food. It's meant not to dominate or overshadow the food's flavor, but to enhance the taste and overall experience.

WORD TO THE WISE

 One of the most common questions I get about engaging in video meetings is whether we should leave our camera on if others have theirs off. Staring at a black box while being the only one on camera can feel jarring, but the short answer is yes—leave it on. This is especially important if we are trying to build rapport with others. Because while it may feel terribly bizarre, as if it's a one-way relationship, we have to remind ourselves that we should leverage all the cues we can give—our facial expressions, our hand movements, and our overall body language—to become more memorable in the viewer's eyes. When people see us, they feel like they recognize us. This creates a familiarity and a stronger impression, which can give us that extra connection point.

THE BOTTOM LINE

- For those of us raised with Quiet Culture values, being in tune with other people's body language comes naturally, but when it comes to utilizing it ourselves, it can quickly fall to the wayside.

- Body language shapes people's perception of our communication ability more than our words or our tone.

- Certain cultures may discourage direct eye contact, especially when power dynamics are present. However, research shows people generally find it attractive when the speaker makes eye contact with them.

- If we're speaking to convince, persuade, sell, or pitch, genuinely smiling will attract people.

- Our hands can be an overlooked communication asset, but if we intentionally use them by holding, pointing, or showcasing something, we can make our speaking more impactful.

- A straight posture can give the perception of confidence, and it can make us *feel* more confident.

FINAL THOUGHTS

Much of this book is anchored in practices I've learned as a TV journalist. It's amazing to see how many powerful and subtle communication techniques can be taken from the industry and applied to the professional world. However, one thing I have not shared is that while starting out as a journalist, I was taught to tell the stories, not *be* the story. In some ways, being a journalist was comforting because I got to ask the questions, so I didn't need to talk about my own insecurities. I could hide my deep-seated struggles and frustrations and avoid exposing how I really felt at work. In fact, the biggest challenge in writing this book was taking off that mask, letting down my styled on-camera hair, and sharing my most vulnerable and even embarrassing moments of being overshadowed and overlooked at work. Because despite knowing what to do and how to do it, it wasn't always smooth sailing. Sometimes I was my own biggest critic, telling myself that my thoughts didn't matter as long as I did good work. In writing this book, I even had moments when I wondered if any of it was worth sharing—which, ironically, is what this book is all about. It's not just about doing the work; it is about *building visibility* around the work; that is, sharing it with others along the way.

One of the beauties in creating the constructs of Quiet Culture and Loud Culture is that I have felt more connected with people than ever before. I have discovered there are *so many* people who struggle with balancing the duality of both worlds. It may seem counterintuitive, but in talking about feeling invisible and stuck at work, you actually start to feel more visible, because you know you're not alone.

So, for my fellow Quiet Culture readers who feel like they are always living within the tension between these two cultures, know that this book is for you. Being seen exactly the way you want to be is possible, and I will be your biggest cheerleader as you find new ways toward better advocating for yourself and your ideas at work. I want to see you sit in meetings where you now know how to strategically speak up. I want to see you take the work you're doing and highlight it to showcase yourself in the best possible light. I want to see you create opportunities for yourself and pitch your ideas confidently. I want to see you revel in your wins and not feel guilty about it. Reframing, being strategic, and communicating effectively are all tactics that can help you ease that confusion about what to do and how to do it. I have intentionally organized this book so that if you ever need inspiration or a specific communication technique to help you prepare for your next meeting, you can quickly turn to the right page and then apply what you've learned.

My other hope in writing this book is that it'll be a catalyst for a bigger conversation around the various ways people show up and engage in the workplace. Just because someone is more quiet doesn't mean they are less capable, involved, or present. In fact, it's the opposite. Those raised with Quiet Culture values are more than capable of making a profound impact on the team and on projects they're working on, as long as they're not treated like they are invisible. So, for leaders who want to build a more inclusive team, know that there are different ways people engage, spend time, handle wins, and manage conflict, much of which is shaped in our earliest years. Acknowledging this diversity is how we can create a better workplace for all.

As we finish up, know this: the ability to get noticed at work for all the right reasons is already in us. We don't have to change ourselves to fit into a loud working world; we just have to be smart about how we show up and how we communicate. The result? Carrying ourselves with ease in *all* environments in front of *all* people. And no matter what, if we stumble or fall along the way, know that we just have to find the courage to try. Everything in here is meant to elevate the person you are, because you absolutely deserve to be heard and seen. In fact, I am doing this work along with you. When we do it together, we are showcasing the power of those raised in a Quiet Culture.

APPRECIATION

As I near the end of writing this book, I cannot help but feel immense gratitude for my army of supporters. It took nearly five years of work, from a seed of an idea to the book you're now holding in your hands. There were too many days and sleepless nights when I wondered if I would get to the finish line, but finally, here we are.

This book would not have been possible without my brilliant editor, Megan McCormack. Thank you for believing in me and in this idea, and for elevating this book to what it is today. I appreciate your confidence in me and how you challenged me to think bigger. It was my dream to broaden the book's theme, and to include more people who might relate to this topic. You single-handedly made that possible with your thoughtful questions and encouragement. Thank you to Niki Papadopoulos and Adrian Zackheim for supporting this book and for your contributions and expertise, which helped crystallize its message. I particularly enjoyed our conversations about Quiet Cultures and Loud Cultures, which led us to name this very real, but not often discussed, workplace construct. To Susette Brooks: your encouraging letter sent after reading my manuscript meant so much to me—more than you'll know. This book could not have found a better home than with Portfolio. Thank you to all at Penguin Random House for bringing it to life.

To my literary agent, Rachel Ekstrom Courage: from the moment we met, I knew we were going to have a ball working together. Thank you for seeing the potential of this book, for championing it, and for guiding me through this process. I am lucky to have you on my side, and I continue to learn so much from you about the publishing industry.

Special thanks to my earliest supporters, who helped me put pen to paper. To my first editor, Danielle Goodman: you understood the vision of this book and you signed on to help me when my mind was still a mess of disparate ideas. To Peter Guzzardi: your critique seeded the idea of where I should take this book, even before I gave myself the permission to do it. Thank you to Ariel Hubbard, who helped me refine what was a very raw manuscript chapter by chapter. And to my dedicated researchers, Alexander Stump and Ridhi Aggarwal: thank you for digging out the golden nuggets to support the book's content. To Leslie Kwoh: your thoughts and critique are so valued. Your feedback is very much echoed in these pages. Joscelyn Daguna and Helena Wong, thank you both for your amazing friendship and for the kindest thoughts on how to make this manuscript and its design better. To Ashley Hong, who supported this idea from the very beginning, and to the Soulcast Media team: thank you for holding down the fort.

To all the people I interviewed for this book: Amy Goodman, Amy Tu, Angela Jia Kim, Anne Mok, Ann Miura-Ko, Audrey Lo, Cheryl Cheng, Don Liu, Edna Ma, Gloria Lee, Jamie Chung, Jerry Kang, Kim Scott, Kristen Taylor, Linda Akutagawa, Lung-Nien Lee, Megan W., Mei Mei, Michael Chen, Monica Lee, Nanxi Liu, Richard Liu, Sandra Liu, Song Richardson, Tatiana Kolovou, Tope Folarin, and Wilson Chu. Thank you for carving out the time to talk about your communication growth and your career lessons. While I couldn't include all the stories and anecdotes, know that every conversation influenced the message of this book in ways big and small. Your advice and insight are in these pages, which will now help readers who grew up with Quiet Culture values find a "smart" way of showing up in the workplace.

Writing a book is such a strange journey. It's a lonely process filled with an incredible amount of self-doubt, yet it's also the most rewarding because of the brilliant people you meet along the way. I have loved making so many new author friends, particularly, Elaine Lin Hering. Your kindness and support mean everything, and I am so happy we're on this journey together.

Finally, my family. Thank you to my mother, the glue that holds our family together. Your selflessness is unmatched and your support of me, often in the quietest of ways, doesn't go unnoticed. Thank you for giving me the time to focus on this work. To my brother, Eric Chen: I am so grateful for our bond.

We started our respective businesses at the same time, and it has been inspiring to see you grow. Thank you for being the best listener and allowing me to be my truest self. To my father: your entrepreneurial spirit is why I do what I do. You seeded the idea that we can all go out and create our own path. To Carter: I love you so much and am so grateful to be your mom. You have filled my heart with so much happiness. You will always be Mama's boy. And finally, to my husband, KaWing. Thank you for being so incredibly understanding of my book-writing journey. You could have probably done without the constant clicking of the keyboard as I wrote into the wee hours of the night, but your support and patience have helped me get this book to the finish line. Thank you for allowing me to be me.

I would not have been able to reach more than two million learners if people had not taken a chance on me as a speaker and an instructor from the very beginning. I am grateful to the institutions that have implemented our work, and to the organizations that have onboarded us as professional development training. I am grateful to the companies that have invited me to speak to their global audience to share the message of building visibility and influence in a way that's smart, not loud.

NOTES

CHAPTER 1: FRICTION AT WORK

9 **corporate workplaces tend to reward:** "Hobbes, Locke, Montesquieu, and Rousseau on Government," *Bill of Rights in Action* 20, no. 2 (2004), Constitutional Rights Foundation, https://www.crf-usa.org/bill-of-rights-in-action/bria-20-2-c-hobbes-locke-montesquieu-and-rousseau-on-government.html.

10 **Amazon's core leadership principles:** "Leadership Principles," Amazon, accessed November 13, 2023, https://www.amazon.jobs/content/en/our-workplace/leadership-principles.

10 **"Debate then commit":** "We're Making Work Meaningful for Everyone, Everywhere," Gusto, accessed November 13, 2023, https://gusto.com/about.

10 **"Be Bold and Move Fast":** "See What It's Like inside Enova," Enova, accessed November 13, 2023, https://www.enova.com/culture.

10 **help others solve problems:** Adam Bryant, "Google's Quest to Build a Better Boss," *New York Times*, March 12, 2011, https://www.nytimes.com/2011/03/13/business/13hire.html.

10 **first-mover advantage:** Jeffrey Pfeffer and Robert I. Sutton, "Evidence-Based Management," *Harvard Business Review*, January 2006, https://hbr.org/s2006/01/evidence-based-management#:~:text=Research%20by%20Wharton%27s%20Lisa%20Bolton,a%20big%20advantage%20over%20competitors.

11 **organizational socialization:** John Van Maanen and Edgar H. Schein, "Toward a Theory of Organizational Socialization," *Research in Organizational Behavior* 1, no. 1 (1977): 209–64.

13 **babble hypothesis:** Natalie Marchant, "People Who Speak More Are More Likely to Be Considered Leaders," World Economic Forum, August 9, 2021, https://www.weforum.org/agenda/2021/08/leaders-talk-more-babble -hypothesis.

19 **According to developmental psychologists:** Albert Bandura, *Social Learning Theory* (Hoboken, NJ: Prentice-Hall, 1977).

CHAPTER 2: THE FOUR CULTURAL REFRAMES

29 **enhances mutual understanding:** N. Simmons-Mackie, "Communication Partner Training in Aphasia: Reflections on Communication Accommodation Theory," *Aphasiology* 32, no. 10 (2018): 1135–44.

30 **people judge others:** A. E. Abele and S. Bruckmüller, "The Bigger One of the 'Big Two'? Preferential Processing of Communal Information," *Journal of Experimental Social Psychology* 47, no. 5 (2011): 935–48, https://doi .org/10.1016/j.jesp.2011.03.028.

30 **positive impression:** W. Rollett, H. Bijlsma, and S. Röhl, eds., *Student Feedback on Teaching in Schools: Using Student Perceptions for the Development of Teaching and Teachers* (New York: Springer, 2021).

34 **management consultants:** Victor Cheng, "What Interviewers Notice in a Consulting Case Interview," CaseInterview.com, https://caseinterview .com/what-interviewers-notice-consulting-case-interview.

36 **"halo effect":** A. Ries, "Understanding Marketing Psychology and the Halo Effect," *Ad Age*, April 17, 2006.

40 **better interpersonal relationships:** J. J. Exline and A. L. Geyer, "Perceptions of Humility: A Preliminary Study," *Self and Identity* 3, no. 2 (2004): 95–114, https://doi.org/10.1080/13576500342000077.

41 **moral elevation:** J. Haidt, "Elevation and the Positive Psychology of Morality," in *Flourishing: Positive Psychology and the Life Well-Lived*, ed. C. L. M. Keyes and J. Haidt (Washington, DC: American Psychological Association, 2003), 275–89, https://doi.org/10.1037/10594-012.

41 **positive organizational outcomes:** M. Vianello, E. M. Galliani, and J. Haidt, "Elevation at Work: The Effects of Leaders' Moral Excellence," *Journal of Positive Psychology* 5, no. 5 (2010): 390–411, https://doi.org/10.1080/174 39760.2010.516764.

43 **transformative mediation:** R. A. B. Bush and J. P. Folger, *The Promise of Mediation: Responding to Conflict through Empowerment and Recognition* (Hoboken, NJ: Jossey-Bass, 1994).

44 **priming them:** Daniel C. Molden, "Understanding Priming Effects in Social Psychology: What Is 'Social Priming' and How Does It Occur?" *Social Cognition* 32, suppl. (2014): 1–11.

CHAPTER 3: OVERCOMING THE QUIET CULTURE BIAS

53 **intersectional invisibility:** B. Bhattacharyya and J. L. Berdahl, "Do You See Me? An Inductive Examination of Differences between Women of Color's Experiences of and Responses to Invisibility at Work," *Journal of Applied Psychology* 108, no. 7 (2023): 1073–95, https://doi.org/10.1037/apl0001072.

58 **we get feedback:** Matthew Solan, "Slowing Down Racing Thoughts," *Harvard Health Publishing*, March 13, 2023, https://www.health.harvard.edu/blog/slowing-down-racing-thoughts-202303132901.

65 **feel hopeful about our progress:** C. K. Y. Chan et al., "What Are the Essential Characteristics for Curriculum Design to Engage Asian Students in Developing Their Self-confidence?" *Curriculum and Teaching* 35, no. 2 (2020): 25–44.

CHAPTER 4: SHAPING OUR CAREER BRAND

74 **affective commitment:** X. Xiaohong and S. C. Payne, "Quantity, Quality, and Satisfaction with Mentoring: What Matters Most?" *Journal of Career Development* 41, no. 6 (2014): 507–25.

75 **"in our lives":** Brené Brown, *Dare to Lead* (New York: Random House, 2018), 189.

76 **read through the list:** Humanists@Work, Work Values Inventory, https://humwork.uchri.org/wp-content/uploads/2015/01/Workvalues-inventory-3.pdf.

CHAPTER 5: BUILDING CREDIBILITY

95 *low* **power-distance cultures:** Kate Sweetman, "In Asia, Power Gets in the Way," *Harvard Business Review*, April 10, 2012, https://hbr.org/2012/04/in-asia-power-gets-in-the-way.

96 **trust and respect:** J. M. Kouzes and B. Z. Posner, *Credibility: How Leaders Gain and Lose It, Why People Demand It* (Hoboken, NJ: Jossey-Bass, 2011).

105 **context surrounding the situation:** Alan C. Mikkelson, David Sloan, and Cris J. Tietsort, "Employee Perceptions of Supervisor Communication Competence and Associations with Supervisor Credibility," *Communication Studies* 72, no. 4 (2021): 600–17, https://doi.org/10.1080/10510974.2021.1953093.

CHAPTER 6: ADVOCATING FOR OURSELVES

125 **"you've told them":** Erin Meyer, *The Culture Map* (New York: Public-Affairs, 2015), 35.

125 **misconstrued as flexible:** M. Liu, "Verbal Communication Styles and Culture," *Oxford Research Encyclopedia of Communication*, November 22, 2016, https://oxfordre.com/communication/view/10.1093/acrefore/9780 190228613.001.0001/acrefore-9780190228613-e-162.

130 **prevention-focused:** E. T. Higgins, "Promotion and Prevention: Regulatory Focus as a Motivational Principle," *Advances in Experimental Social Psychology* 30 (1998): 1–46, https://doi.org/10.1016/S0065-2601(08) 60381-0.

131 **based on their style:** Heidi Grant and E. Tory Higgins, "Do You Play to Win—or to Not Lose?" *Harvard Business Review*, March 2013, https://hbr .org/2013/03/do-you-play-to-win-or-to-not-lose.

132 **factor of ten:** Kotter Contributor, "Think You're Communicating Enough? Think Again," *Forbes*, June 14, 2011, https://www.forbes.com /sites/johnkotter/2011/06/14/think-youre-communicating-enough -think-again/?sh=3819d36275eb.

CHAPTER 7: MAXIMIZING OUR WORDS

163 **we speak to persuade:** Carmine Gallo, "The Art of Persuasion Hasn't Changed in 2,000 Years," *Harvard Business Review*, July 15, 2019, https:// hbr.org/2019/07/the-art-of-persuasion-hasnt-changed-in-2000-years.

170 **of the pause:** S. Liu et al., "How Pause Duration Influences Impressions of English Speech: Comparison between Native and Non-native Speakers," *Frontiers in Psychology* 13 (2022), https://doi.org/10.3389/fpsyg.2022 .778018.

172 **Nerves and performance:** K. H. Teigen, "Yerkes-Dodson: A Law for all Seasons," *Theory and Psychology* 4, no. 4 (1994): 525–47, https://doi.org /10.1177/0959354394044004.

CHAPTER 8: EXPANDING OUR TONE OF VOICE

186 **five tonal elements:** Wendy DeLeo LeBorgne, "Beyond Words: How Your Voice Shapes Your Communication Image," *Remodista* (blog), June 25, 2020, https://www.remodista.com/blog/beyond-words-how-your-voice -shapes-your-communication-image.

200 **increased uptalk:** "The Unstoppable March of the Upward Inflection?" *BBC News*, August 11, 2014, https://www.bbc.com/news/magazine -28708526.

CHAPTER 9: UTILIZING OUR BODY LANGUAGE

207 **only 7 percent:** E. S. Berscheid, "Review of Silent Messages: Implicit Communication of Emotions and Attitudes. 2nd ed.," *PsycCRITIQUES* 26, no. 8 (1981): 648, https://doi.org/10.1037/020475.

210 **"quick first impression":** New York University, "Scientists Identify Neural Circuitry of First Impressions," *ScienceDaily*, March 13, 2009, www.sciencedaily.com/releases/2009/03/090308142247.htm.

210 **seven seconds:** Carol Kinsey Goman, "Seven Seconds to Make a First Impression," *Forbes*, February 13, 2011, https://www.forbes.com/sites/carolkinseygoman/2011/02/13/seven-seconds-to-make-a-first-impression/?sh=45fa8a272722.

211 **makes eye contact:** C. A. Conway et al., "Evidence for Adaptive Design in Human Gaze Preference," *Proceedings of the Royal Society B: Biological Sciences* 275, no. 1630 (2008): 63–69, http://doi.org/10.1098/rspb.2007.1073.

213 **happier faces:** Y. Dong et al., "Effects of Facial Expression and Facial Gender on Judgment of Trustworthiness: The Modulating Effect of Cooperative and Competitive Settings," *Frontiers in Psychology* 9 (2018): 2022, https://doi.org/10.3389/fpsyg.2018.02022.

216 **comprehend our message:** Autumn B. Hostetter, "When Do Gestures Communicate? A Meta-analysis," *Psychological Bulletin* 137, no. 2 (2011): 297–315, https://doi.org/10.1037/a0022128.

218 **feel about ourselves:** Sarah L. Arnette and Terry F. Pettijohn II, "The Effects of Posture on Self-Perceived Leadership," *International Journal of Business and Social Science* 3, no. 14 (2012): 8–13, https://ijbssnet.com/journals/Vol_3_No_14_Special_Issue_July_2012/2.pdf.

218 **head of the table:** Arnette and Pettijohn, "The Effects of Posture on Self-Perceived Leadership."

INDEX